The LUCKY PIGEON

THE TRUE ADVENTURES OF A YOUNG CANADIAN AIRMAN DURING WORLD WAR II

By

JOHN A. NEAL

T0098525

TURNER PUBLISHING COMPANY

TURNER PUBLISHING COMPANY

Copyright © 1997 John A. Neal
Publishing Rights: Turner Publishing Company.
This book or any part thereof may not be reproduced
without the written consent of the author and publisher.

Turner Publishing Company Staff:
Editor: Herbert C. Banks II
Designer: Holly Jo Coleman

Library of Congress Catalog Card No.
97-60400

ISBN: 978-1-68162-180-7

Limited Edition. Additional copies may be
purchased directly from the publisher.

TABLE OF CONTENTS

Foreword

8 February 1944 — Mission: Frankfurt, Germany

Maximum effort under adverse conditions of weather, rendezvous timing and loss of fighter coverage led to early enemy air attacks on route to target. All this accompanied by accurate anti-aircraft actions. German fighters quickly singled out "tail-end Charlies" and were able to effectively make nose attacks, which resulted in killing our bombardier, wounding and incapacitating myself (the navigator) and causing a fire in the bomb bay and right wing.

John A. (Jack) Kupsick, Navigator 8th U.S. Air Force

The order to bail out soon was given. Due to equipment shortages, I had a bastardized parachute set-up of an American harness and a British chest pack, which only would fit on the harness rings one way: by putting the "D-ring" handles on my left side. Since that arm and hand had been hit with a number of fragments of an enemy 20mm cannon round, I had to jam my wounded hand into the D-ring before I jumped. Needless to say, after diving head-first out of the forward hatch, the weight of my hand and arm popped the chute at altitude.

Fortunately, I fell through several layers of cloud, so I was not pursued or shot at while I descended — which was happening to others at the time. I did have some anxious moments, however, as my chute collapsed six times on the way down. Suffice it to say I was relieved that it re-opened each time and finally stayed open until I touched down, which was as easy as stepping off a chair.

As I landed, a civilian ran up and helped me unbuckle, since my wounded hand and arm were not cooperating. I had lost my right boot and heated shoe, so we put my left boot on my right foot, and I took off running with two "left" feet. The civilian in turn took off in the opposite direction with my "silk umbrella to safety." I lost my D-ring and never collected a Caterpillar, but a parachute saved my life and led to freedom via the French Underground.

Fifty-plus years of action and events have not dimmed the memory of tense moments, and hours spent evading the enemy after being shot down over German-held territory during World War II. In this book, John Neal has graphically painted a word picture of his escape and evasion experience, some 90 days of which we shared. He, a Royal Canadian Air Force bombardier; a Canadian navigator, Bob Lindsay; and myself, an American B-17 navigator, were hidden together by the French Underground in the home of a Belgian couple who were operating a farm in Occupied France.

Our ultimate return to Allied control was due to the bravery, dedication and patriotic action of many citizens of the Allies. We three owe a profound debt of gratitude to the French, Belgian and Dutch civilians who risked all to save us and thus thwart the enemy. The contents of this book, and others like it, should be required reading for present and future generations. It depicts the actions of true patriots.

John A. Kupsick
LtCol., USAF (Ret.)

An Introduction

The group of older men were gathered around the large tables in the dining room at Mewata Armory in downtown Calgary. They were holding the weekly luncheon meeting of the Southern Alberta branch of the Aircrew Association. All of the men were retired Airmen, having left their flying days far behind; most of them hadn't even been near a cockpit since the end of the war.

Author John A. Neal, "the Birdman of Fish Creek."

But that didn't stop them all from talking about it! That was the main purpose behind the Association, and the luncheons every week; to talk about the old days when they were wearing the Air Force blue, and flying through the wild blue yonder. If the stories told were believable, those men were all the greatest of heroes.

And those men were heroes, although few of them might be wearing major decorations. Just by learning their trades well, doing their duty to their country, and returning safely home, they were the heroes that war produces.

With lunch finally over, the conversation naturally turned to the subject, "What did you do during the war? Tell us about it." Someone would be called on to relate his tale — where he trained, where he served, what happened to him, and what he had done since. The discussion would last for another hour and then break up, each going his separate way. Next week, at the same time and the same place, it would happen all over again.

Time after time, somebody would ask, "Why don't we write these stories down for history? Unless this is done, all of these adventures will die, along with us." Some old airmen, and a few interested authors, have taken this warning seriously, and many air adventures have flooded the book stores since. The following is just one more piece of history, and an attempt to record the author's career while wearing the Air Force blue. The story starts out on a cold day in March 1942, and winds up on another cold day in November 1945.

No attempts have been made to make the story any more heroic than it turned out to be; it is merely an account of the author's life as it evolved during those days. An account of the successes, the disappointments, the joys, the failures, the terrors, and of course, the temptations, that were encountered. With the writing starting in his senior years, and mostly from memory, there are bound to be some errors or omissions. For these sins of the aging memory banks, the author must beg your forgiveness.

Throughout the first part of the story, there are included a number of comments placed in parentheses. Mostly these are assessments made by instructors or superiors during the different phases of the training. Others were made by the author himself in order to justify his own evaluation of his status as an airman in good standing. In some cases, it was not "In Good Standing."

But on to the story! Try to visualize a locomotive repair shop, on a cold day in March 1942. Massive steam locomotives were standing side by side in varying stages of repair. About a dozen young, dirty-faced apprentices, who really should have been working, were gathered inside one of the boilers to talk. The subject, as usual, was the war....

So, on to Chapter 1!

THE MAKING OF THE AIRMAN

On April 29, 1940, the governments of Canada, Great Britain, Australia and New Zealand got together in Ottawa to sign an agreement implementing the "British Commonwealth Air Training Plan." The Plan, as it came to be known, was formulated to supply the huge requirements for aircrew which the governments felt would be required for World War II.

Shortly after the signing of the agreement, several other members of the Empire came on board, including South Africa, Southern Rhodesia and India. Even the Bahamas established one air station to be used in the training of airmen. Then, by agreement with the United States of America, five stations were opened in that country. These were used to train airmen from the Empire, but mostly flyers from Great Britain.

A few details of this Plan are in order, just to show how much importance the Allies placed on defeating Hitler from the air.

During the life of the Plan, the stations used in the training totaled 333, and the number of airmen trained exceeded 300,000. The distribution of these stations and airmen in training, among the various countries involved, is shown as follows: (from "A Time for Courage," by John Terraine. The Royal Air Force in the European War, 1939-1945).

	Stations	Trainees
Canada	92	137,739
United Kingdom	153	88,022
Australia	26	27,387
South Africa	25	24,184
South. Rhodesia	10	10,033
India	9	-
New Zealand	6	5,609
Middle East	6	-
U.S.A.	5	10,000+
Totals	333	303,604

In his book, "Aerodrome of Democracy," F.J. Hatch lists a total of 131,553 Canadian-born airmen that trained in Canada between October 1940 and March 1945. Another 5,296 were trained prior to October 1940, for a grand total of 136,849. These were broken down as follows:

Pilots	- 53,947	Nav. B	- 9,795
Nav. W	- 4,449	Observers	- 1,006
Navigators	- 15,870	Bomb Aimers	- 15,673
WO/AG	- 18,496	Air Gunners	- 14,996
Naval AG's	- 704	Flt. Engineers	- 1,913

Hatch lists 105 flying training schools of various types, as compared to the 92 listed by Terraine. As in all air war ventures, there were negative factors at work; many men died in training as well as in combat. A total of 856 airmen died in Canada from flying accidents between 1940 and 1945. Broken down by the country of origin, these casualties are as follows:

Royal Australian Air Force	-	65
Royal Air Force	-	291
Royal Canadian Air Force	-	469
Royal New Zealand Air Force	-	31
Total	-	<u>856</u>

A more recent volume, compiled by Les Allison and Harry Hayward at the Brandon, Man., Air Museum and titled, "They Shall Grow Not Old," is even more disturbing. It contains the names of over 18,000 Canadian airmen killed in action, killed in training, or died from natural causes. Our air casualties, during WWII, were over 13 percent — huge losses of our best young manhood!

Not to be forgotten in any written praise of the Plan are the many thousands of airmen trained for careers on the ground. For every plane that flew, there were aero engine mechanics, aero frame mechanics, armament technicians, radar specialists, flying control specialists, etc. Without them, we would not even have gotten off the ground. Looking to our well-being were the many cooks, clerks, medical personnel, drivers, barbers and all those lovely WDs who so gracefully parried our advances. But most of all, the instructors — who, though diligently helping see us on our way, were mostly destined for little glory on the battlefield.

No. 1 Bombing and Gunnery School, Jarvis, Ontario, Class of Nov. 22, 1942, to Feb. 20, 1943. Shown from left are (front row) C.H. Balsdon, J.E. McGowan, author J.A. Neal, H.C. Mallette*, J.D. McCreary*, Ron Smalley*, Chas. Panton*, C. Szymanski*, J.G. Shaw, (back row) Eric Cutler*, R.B. Atkinson, E.B. Murphy, S.M. Preston*, G.A. Walker, A.E. Schorn, H. Trueman*, Jim Hynds, J.W. Cockburn. (*Denotes killed in action.)

The writer was one of the 300,000. The first part of the story proceeds from the recruitment centre, through the many training stations, and then overseas to put all this training to use.

Notes:

Many of the airmen listed as "Canadian" were actually flyers who had come over the border from the U.S.A. to join the RCAF. They probably make up the difference between John Terraine's figures for Canadians and F.J. Hatch's. Most of these were before Pearl Harbor, but they still came after, mainly because they were not allowed to fly in the U.S. Air Force. Many of them are listed in "They Shall Grow Not Old."

Chapter 1

THE RECRUIT

This diary, if an account of my wartime activities it could be called, started out on a cold day in March 1942. At the time, I was employed as a machinist apprentice with the Canadian National Railways, working on repairs to steam locomotives at the shops in Point St. Charles, part of Montreal. This was to have been my chosen career, as had the railways been for so many of my family.

But World War II was really beginning to come home to the people during this period. The Japanese had attacked Pearl Harbor three months earlier, and the United States was now in the war. Many veterans, already returned home from the wars, were telling us about the glories to be gained on foreign shores, or in foreign skies. More than once we civilians were asked, by strangers on the street, why we were not in uniform. The apprentices were beginning to question our true contribution to the war effort.

Our usual conversations were about the glories of wearing a uniform, whether in the land, sea or air forces. All of us knew where we would eventually be serving, but it took a suspicious, and prying, works manager to finally propel us into taking action.

03/12/42	Montreal	Enlistment	#13 Recruiting Depot

("He is keen to fly. Alert. Two years of high school but no physics. Looks fair. He is material for aircrew with D.P.Y.T. course. Suitability for commission — none").

Patriotism and bravery had very little to do with it at the time! Joining up in 1942 may have looked as if it was the thing to do, but only the immediate risk to my job precipitated me into taking the action when I did. Having barely turned 18, I had not given a lot of thought to when I would join up.

There were about 10 of us on that cold March afternoon in 1942; we were goofing off from other, more serious things that needed to be done. Sprawled all over the inside of the gutted locomotive boiler, our conversation was, as usual, the war that had been raging for 2 1/2 years in Europe. There was little thought to the work for which we were being paid.

Suddenly the cover over the entrance to the boiler flew off, and into our haven climbed the works manager, Mr. Melanson. Looking around at us, he said, "I want all of you in my office in one half hour." Sheepishly facing him around his desk, he said, "You guys have two options; get out of here and join up, or get out of here and find another line of work. You're no good to me as you are. Get this war out of your systems, and then come back so I can get some useful work out of you." Right after supper that same night, I went out, telling nobody where I was going, and headed for the recruiting centre.

I was going into the Royal Canadian Air Force — there was little doubt in my mind about that. After a year in the part-time Ordinance Corps, there was no way I was going to spend my war years doing locomotive repairs on foreign shores. A few of my old high school chums were already flying Spitfires, and that was the life I wanted.

So, on that cold March evening I traveled by tram to Bishop Street, the site of the Montreal recruiting centre. Without a lot of serious thought about what I was doing, I went in and applied for enlistment. A very attractive young lady, Mlle. Lachapelle, recorded my details, as well as giving me the first positive view of what I was getting into. This was, however, the first of the humorous occurrences to plague me during my time in the forces.

I had just recently acquired a new denture plate. During my conversation with Mlle. Lachapelle, the plate flew out of my mouth, to the mirth of all those around us. To ease my embarrassment, the lady commented that I should have waited a little longer; the Air Force would have paid for the plate. But she refused any idea of retroactivity.

I remember blowing the mercury up the tube to prove that I was fit enough for aircrew. Surely had there been just one more notch to reach, I would certainly have lost out on my ambition to be a flyer. But, as it turned out, I did pass all of my medical tests with flying colours. And, thankfully so, since there was some pressure on me, given my work background, to enlist as an aeroengine mechanic.

When I returned home that night, I told my parents what I had done, and that I would be going into the Air Force. I don't believe that I had ever seen my mother fly into such a passion, over any action I had ever taken, until then. Her tears fell like the water over Niagara Falls. For hours my father and I tried to placate her, with little success. I was apparently the great hope of the family, and here I was going away to be killed

Neal on a park bench in Bournemouth, June 1943.

for certain. Later actions during my flying career almost proved her right!

Before I could be sworn into the Air Force, I needed to go to the University of Montreal to take the Dominion Provincial Youth Training course. This was designed to upgrade my current grade-nine education to aircrew standards. The conscription debate was then underway, and we trainees were urged to stay clear of the full-time students. They were mostly French-speaking, and not too happy about the prospects of serving in the armed forces. Very fortunately, no major confrontations occurred at the university, and we finished all our studies by late May. We were now ready for the blue uniforms that we had been waiting for.

Notes:

We had to blow a column of mercury up a tube to prove that we had the lung capacity for high altitude flying.

Chapter 2

THE TRAINEE

<u>**05/26/42**</u>   **<u>Montreal</u>**   **<u>Swearing-in</u>**   **<u>#13 Recruiting Depot</u>**

About a dozen raw recruits stood in a circle at the recruiting centre and swore allegiance to King George VI, our new Commander in Chief. I was now Airman 2nd Class John A. Neal, with regimental number of R-164712, and about the greenest airman the Airforce then possessed. We were all then trucked off to the Lachine Manning Depot, just west of Montreal, with little more than the clothes on our backs.

Our first sight there was of thousands of blue-clad Airmen, marching everywhere, and the large gray barrack blocks where we would be living. Other than that, things did not look all that promising; there were no airplanes to be seen anywhere!

<u>**05/26/42**</u>   **<u>Lachine</u>**   **<u>Start of Training</u>**   **<u>#5 Manning Depot</u>**

(Making an Airman out of me, but I was never certain if that ever did succeed)

Firstly we were given our uniforms (they sort of fit, if one bent over the right way) and then came the T.A.B.T. shots (many of us fainted, but I was one of the fortunate few who survived the day). The following day brought the after-effects, and we were confined to our beds. After this came the drill, drill and more drill. Life became one long march after another. If not this, then it was double time. As we became accustomed to the drill square, a certain pride began to take over our efforts. We would prove that we could be good, disciplined Airmen, even if the effort was going to kill us.

There was a precision squad at Lachine, composed of Airmen who had shown a high degree of skill on the parade square. They traveled around eastern Canada and the U.S., showing off this skill as advertising for the RCAF. Most of us hoped to be chosen for this squad, and worked hard to merit the choice. But few were chosen, and most of us went on to the following stages in our training.

Three events during my stay at Lachine really stood out in my memory. The first was the night I was assigned to guard duty at the back gate. During the duty, I challenged the base CO while he was in civilian clothes. He assumed that I should have known him in any attire. This was my first experience in being severely disciplined since the last time I was called to the principal's office. Then there was another day when I spilled drinks all over the executive officer and his friends while I was serving as waiter in the officer's mess. This was probably the shortest career as waiter in recorded history.

Then there was the night that I slipped under the fence while the Blue Bells troupe was playing on the base. The CO had wanted a full turnout for this group of entertainers, and confined us all to base to assure this. Of all the guys who slipped out, I was naturally the last to try, and naturally the first to be caught. My penalty was seven days confined to barracks, and plenty of KP duty, hopefully to keep me away from further trouble while in uniform. Unfortunately, it did not always work, as later events in my career will show.

Lachine was a dry town in those days, and so we had to search diligently to find any sort of refreshment when off base. However, we did locate one restaurant that served a special kind of tea, in an attractive teapot and with fine chinaware. However, the contents were more likely to have been made by Seagram than by Salada.

Somewhere around late July, we were sufficiently trained in the basics of discipline to go on to the next stage of airmanship. A number of us who needed further schooling in math and science were posted to Quebec City, where a forces school was located. I was able to call home and let them know I was leaving, and when. Sure enough, Mom showed up at Westmount railway station just as we were boarding and had to kiss her "Baby" good-bye — right in front of all his new buddies!

07/17/42	Quebec City	Math & Science	#4 Manning Depot

(65 percent on math and 84 percent on science)

The #4 Manning Depot occupied a vacated nunnery in lower town, right alongside Victoria Park. We lived and studied in the same gray stone building, but in a city with the nature of Quebec, we were not all destined to be quite so celibate as the previous residents.

The boardwalk in upper town was a great place for chasing the ladies. Unfortunately, I had to work hard to keep up my marks, and was only able to spend a little time on the prowl. But this did provide enough memories to remember Quebec City as a fine posting.

We were not very well-liked in some parts of the city, and many airmen came home somewhat the worse for wear. At least one of our chaps sported broken limbs inflicted by local bullies. A friend and I went to a waterfront cafe one day, and were threatened by about five rough-looking chaps. Just as it was getting serious, and we were being hustled outside, another of our friends showed up. With the newcomer standing some 6' 5" high, the bullies considered themselves outnumbered and took off. With a sigh of relief, we finished our meal and returned to the nunnery.

In actuality, we could not completely blame the local males, as we had largely taken over the ladies of the town, leaving few for them.

Long weekend passes were something of a rarity at this stage of training, but I was able to obtain one 72-hour break while in Quebec City. A couple of the trainees, myself included, decided to go to Montreal, but the only transport we were able to secure was an open-backed truck. Climbing on board, we held on all the way, suffering the cool winds of autumn in the process. I had also picked up a large bag of grapes to supply the rations needed during the drive.

With the sour grapes, and the cool winds, most of my leave was spent in bed suffering from a belly ache and a touch of flu. If there was to be a next time,

The leading aircraftsman just after Victoriaville Initial Ground Training School. (Ground-crew types told the girls we wore the white patch because we had VD.)

I would spring for the train. But there was no next time; by the middle of September we finished up our course. With passing marks, I was sent on to the next stage in my training, Initial Training School.

<u>**09/14/42**</u>   <u>**Victoriaville**</u>   <u>**Initial Training**</u>   <u>**#3 I.T.S.**</u>

("Intelligent, eager but could do much better. Character and Leadership - 96. Alternate recommendation - W.A.G. High Altitude - Unsuitable. Position in class - 88th out of 130 [79 percent]).

This school was again an old converted nunnery, with a big field in the back. With Windsor Elementary Flying School not far away, we often had Tiger Moths dropping in on us. Every once in a while, one would touch down in the back field and take off again. For most of us, this was our first sight of a plane, and just enough to make us want to get the course finished, and on with the flying. Many of the students were rewarded with a shot at pilot, but many others had to be content with other aircrew positions.

This was my first encounter with the intense study required to prepare for actual flying: navigation, astronomy, mathematics, aircraft recognition, etc. Most of them I passed successfully, but trying to fly the Link Trainer proved to be my downfall; I kept crashing it. In order to ensure the future safety of the people on the ground and in the air, it was decided that my future lay in jobs other than pilot.

Hence, I was assigned at graduation to a future as observer. A little later this was modified to bomb-aimer. The increasing use of four-engine bombers required that this discipline be split into two categories: navigator and bomb-aimer. The former got us to the target and the latter delivered the bombs.

We were, again, not too well-liked by the townspeople, and for the same reasons as in Quebec. Fortunately, I was only 30 miles from Richmond, Quebec, where we had lived some years before. I spent most of my weekends there and started going out with a few old girl friends from the past.

On graduation from Victoriaville, we all were given our first promotions. We were now Leading Aircraftsmen, and able to sew the coveted propellers onto our sleeves. We now had somebody to boss around: the hapless AC2's!

Notes:

T.A.B.T. shots: *Tetanus Antibiotic Serum.*

KP (Kitchen Police) Detail: *sounds like a fun thing, but it was mostly washing dishes or cleaning garbage cans. Listening to the Blue Bells may have been more pleasant.*

Leading Aircraftsmen: *In the Air Force, this was the equivalent of Lance Corporal or Leading Seaman.*

Chapter 3

THE FLYER

11/23/42   **Jarvis**   **Bombing & Gunnery**   **#1 B&G School**

(Bombing — very good results. Gunnery — had best results in class. Average in classroom. Very good practical worker. Position: #6 in 20. [79.7 percent]. Commission — Suitable.)

Following graduation at Victoriaville and a short leave, I went on to Jarvis to receive my first flight training. Located some 30 miles south of Hamilton, it was a small farmer's town not far from the northern shores of Lake Erie. They had taken some farmer's fields, and carved out an airfield for the British Commonwealth Air Training Plan. By the time of my arrival, there were twin-engine Avro Ansons, to be used in bombing training, and twin-engine Bristol Bolingbrokes, to be used in air-to-air gunnery.

Flying seemed at first very much the romantic exercise, but with one of the coldest winters on record, it soon achieved a damper. Some early bombing exercises were done in such bone-chilling cold that I could not even force the bombsight to move. The gun turrets in the Bolingbrokes froze up so that we could not fire, or at least aim them in the direction we wanted the bullets to go. How I began to miss all of the warm days of Lachine Manning Depot!

Neal during cold-weather training days.

Fortunately, much of our initial gunnery training was done from ground turrets overlooking Lake Erie. The station cook made us a supply of sandwiches, and with these we were bussed out to the site near Nanticote. We spent the day firing round after round out over the lake, hoping, of course, the range was not enough for the bullets to cross to the other shore. Now that the Americans were in the war, we wanted to keep them there. But the winds off the lake chilled all the gunners to the bone.

For bombing training on the ground, we had the tower, which kept some of the cold out. The student lay on his stomach on the second floor while the target, in the form of an image projected from above, passed by below. We followed the track until we reached the target, then dropped a simulated bomb. It was not as effective as bombing from the air, but was a whole lot warmer.

One chilling episode at Jarvis brought home to me the inherent dangers of flying. I was suffering from a rash of boils, which had been one of my curses since childhood. At the request of the station medical officer, I checked into the base hospital for tests. Shortly after getting settled in, a Bolingbroke crashed close to the base, with five aboard. Three airmen were killed instantly, and the other two, in very poor condition, were brought into the same room as I. After a few hours of observing these poor "survivors," I was convinced that self-treatment was better than staying in the hospital. Without waiting for permission, I checked myself out and returned to duty. The boils quickly disappeared.

Christmas 1942 was spent on base except for a little carousing at nearby Simcoe. (Married guys got the time off, but we singles had to wait for New Year's.) But a week later I received leave and headed home by train to Montreal. But before leaving the Hamilton area, I spent my meager military pay on Christmas presents for the family. The purchasing was done at the local Eaton's store, and most of this was done with the help of an attractive young store clerk. Unfortunately, an unromantic store manager prevented me from taking the clerk along as my personal present. Who knows what might have come out of this shopping trip?

The leave at home was quiet, but comforting, and shortly after I was back at Jarvis training as usual. In the aerial bombing, we were usually three students to an exercise, and the bombs were 11 1/2 lb. practice ones. I had the impression that most of mine were landing in the next county. For air gunnery, I often seemed a lot closer to shooting down the drogue-towing Lysander plane, rather than holing the drogue itself. But as my results showed, the exercises were satisfactory, and I was sent on to my next posting: air observer school.

02/22/43	Malton	Navigation	#1 Air Observer School

(Air work average. Ground work poor due to lack of attention during lectures. Above-average aircraft recognition. A shifty type of individual. Can bear watching. Could have worked harder. As it was, work was good. Better practical man than theoretical one. Position — #5 in 22 [78 percent]. Assessment — Above average. Commission — unsuitable)

Malton, as most people will know, is the correct name for what is now known as Pearson International Airport. Unfortunately, all evidence of the wartime station was removed during the construction of the present Terminal #1. Malton was a fine station, not many miles away from downtown Toronto, and hopefully our last stop before wearing the wings we all sought.

We were mainly taught navigation here, although other disciplines were given us during our ground classes. We went to classes in the morning and flew in the afternoons or evenings. Since much of our operational flying would be done at night, it was imperative that we have practice in navigation and bombing in the dark. We were given plenty of this.

Most of the practice flights were routine flights around central Ontario (with some bombing thrown in) and we never encountered any major problems, save once. On this occasion, it did appear that my flying career was to be a short one. With staff pilot Zimmerman at the controls, we took off for a cross-country east of Toronto. Almost from take-off, we found ourselves in snow; a blanket of white flakes kept us from seeing anything along the plotted course. We flew on, completely blind, for several hours, following the flight plan but never knowing our exact location.

Finally, when we were getting really concerned about the fuel situation, we decided we had to take action to find out where we were. Flying as close to the ground as possible, we all strained our eyes looking for the vital pin point. Suddenly, after what seemed an eternity, one of the students spotted a small town through a break in the snow. Then we saw a railroad line passing through the town. At almost ground zero, we zoomed by the station where the name of the town showed us to be over Caledon. While we now knew where we were, it did create a little embarrassment; Caledon was north of Toronto, not east where we were supposed to be.

Once our location was determined, we set course for Toronto. We came down out of the blanket of snow at the corner of Bay and Front streets. Abandoning the exercise, we flew home the easy way; up Bay Street, along St. Claire Road, and out the Old Weston Road to Malton. All the way we stayed under 100 feet, with some roofs higher than we were. Well over three hours were spent on this exercise, and we had to do it all over again another day.

The rest of the exercises were routine, and finally we knew enough navigation to at least get around central Ontario. How we would get around overseas would prove to be another matter.

While at Malton, I was only a few miles away from my Uncle Jack's diner in Weston.

Neal, his mother and sister, Dorothy, on the day he received his wings.

So, when the food served on base got really bad, I knew where I could get the best fish and chips around. As the only member of the family then in uniform, I was given a special place at their table. On the base, I started to drink Coca-Cola between morning classes, although I had never been a heavy soft-drink user. On one morning I went through six of these, and found by noon I had a greenish coating on my teeth. Ever after I have had an aversion to Coke, although I would use it to polish my buttons.

Malton was a fine posting, and we were given a fair amount of time off. If not at Uncle Jack's, I spent time in downtown Toronto. One senior lady who lived in a suite at the Royal York hotel opened her doors for any of the young airmen who wanted to come visiting. With everything free, naturally I spent a lot of my time there. But not so much that I couldn't enjoy some of the dances going on in town. And, one or two of the ladies.

On the evening of March 31, 1943, our graduation party was convened. It took place on the top floor of the Royal York. With the ending of our formal training in Canada, the party turned into a rather wild celebration. We all made it to the Wings Parade two days later, but I do not recall it as one of my more alert days. But it was a proud one, as the commanding officer pinned the observer's wing onto my chest. I was now a bonafide flyer! And at that very same moment, promoted to sergeant.

My mother and sister, Dorothy, had attended the Wings Parade. After the parade and a short visit with Uncle Jack and his family, we took the train back to Montreal. I was now on embarkation leave, and getting ready to head overseas to put my training to good use.

04/02/43   Verdun   Embarkation Leave

Sgt. John Neal did not last long! Within the week I was Pilot Officer John Neal. I had made it to the top third of the graduating class, and was one of those to receive a commission. I was quite surprised at the promotion, but at the increased income, I'd take it any way I can get it.

With the brand new wings and stripes (I would have to leave my officer's uniform until I arrived in Halifax), I started on my two weeks' embarkation leave. While spent at home, I had to show it all off to some of my old girl friends, Mr. Melanson at the locomotive shop, and Mr. Grant, principal of my old high school. The latter asked me to give a talk to the Air Cadets, on my life in the RCAF. I did not think that my first 11 months had really been that notable, but the young cadets took it all in.

One of the most satisfying things happening during the leave was the arrival of my call-up papers. They had arrived just one year late, but I thought they should have known I was already in uniform. I took the papers down to the Army Recruiting office and, with a smug smile, told the clerks where they could shove them. Service life had made me bolder!

Part of my class from Victoriaville were still in pilot training at St. Hubert airfield, #13 Service Flying Training School. I went out to visit a few friends and, while there, was asked if I would like a flip in a Harvard. Very innocently I said yes, and was assigned to a sergeant pilot as passenger. We were going up for an instrument check. Well this pilot (nicknamed Sgt. Fearless, and I soon knew why) turned out to be the wildest of the instructor pilots on the base.

Once aloft, he turned around and asked me how I liked my flying. When I asked "What?" he took it for "Wild" and started to show me what he could really do with an airplane. Rolls, stalls, loops, dives, skimming the ground, the fences, the barns, the telephone poles, nothing was sacred that day in the St. Hubert area. When we finally landed, I climbed out gingerly, figuring I was a basket case after all that. But I found that I still had good land legs, and had actually enjoyed the experience. Perhaps, after all, the Air Force had missed out on the chance for one of their better fighter pilots, by making a bomb-aimer out of me.

Finally my leave came to an end, but not before enjoying one last evening of revelry at the Savoy Club. The family saw me off on the train to Halifax, where I was to board my ship for overseas. Mom was quite settled by now on my future role in the air, and the good-byes were much less tearful than the night of my joining up. After an overnight train trip, passing by Quebec city, crossing Gaspe, along the New Brunswick coast, and through Nova Scotia, I arrived in Halifax. This was the location of the Y Depot, my last stop before being posted to foreign shores.

Notes:

Ansons: *a twin engine training airplane, sometimes called "The Greenhouse" because of the many windows in some versions. It was a friendly old plane, and very few trainees came to grief in her.*

Bolingbroke: *a relative of the Blenheim which had come to so much grief over Europe. She also caused much grief during training.*

Chapter 4

THE AIRMAN

(Going overseas. My great adventure is about to begin. How right I was.)

Halifax was the first seaside city I had ever visited; we were basically inlanders and, until joining up, I had thought my future lay anywhere between Montreal and Toronto. But as the Air Force was beginning to show me, there was a whole big world out there to see. With Halifax, I was just getting started.

My first act, after getting settled into the Y depot, was to buy a uniform. Officers were given a $150 allowance to cover clothing, while non-commissioned airmen received theirs free. I did this shopping at the local Eaton's store, and after a few days was decked out as a pilot officer. What a great feeling to be on the receiving end of the salutes for a change! From then on, it was only a matter of waiting until a posting came up for overseas. Mine took seven weeks.

We had a minimum of training while there, and one of the few places we did train was in the tank, a pressure chamber in which they sealed the airmen and took them to a simulated altitude of 35,000 feet. This was meant to test our capacity for high altitude flying. Why they went that high is questionable, since nothing we would fly would go over 25,000 feet.

The one major problem with Halifax is that it was a Navy town; there were far more dark blue uniforms than Air Force blue, or even Army khaki. The harbor, as well as Bedford Basin, was packed with Navy and merchant ships waiting for convoy. With the traditional animosity between Navy and Air Force, we tended to steer clear of one another as much as possible. The exception was one very rash occasion, when good sense was cast aside in favor of a night with the girls.

Frank Berry, of the Royal New Zealand Air Force, and I had become good friends, and were going everywhere together. One evening we went out with a couple of Wrens (Navy Ladies), the one I dated being a friend from home. After dinner and a show, we rashly took them to the Silver Slipper restaurant on Barrington Street. The Navy, with the Silver Slipper as one of their major hangouts, did not really appreciate the gesture. Air Force officers just did not take out Navy Ladies; we were expected to stay with Air Force Ladies.

So the fight started in the booth next to ours, and spilled down the length of the restaurant. They ignored us at first, but we knew they would get around to us in time. Rather than wait for these events to occur, we slipped out and were fortunately able to outrun the Navy, and survive the meeting. From then on, Frank and I stuck to the safer confines of the Y Depot.

After I had been at Halifax for about four weeks, a posting came up with my name on it. I was part of a draft of 75 airmen sailing on a small ship, part of a convoy. I was down with the flu at the time and unable to join the draft. This was most fortunate for me, since the ship was torpedoed in mid-Atlantic, with only 25 airmen surviving. Three weeks later the Louis Pasteur pulled into port, and we were told this was how we would get to England. It was a whole lot bigger than a little mud bucket that needed a convoy!

On the last night of the stay in Halifax, we decided to do it up brown before going on to England.

We started out in the Mess, with the bartender suggesting "Alabama Fog Lifters" as a way to getting a real party going. With one ounce each of gin, rum, scotch and rye, and a pint of beer for a chaser, he certainly knew something we didn't. I only needed one! Then we were invited to a party in town, and I could scarcely remember what went on.

However, I did remember one very special lady, who had hailed from Cobourg, Ontario, but I could not remember if I had made any ungentlemanly passes at her. I had her address, so I wrote on arrival in England, to find out what sins I might have committed. To my relief, I had been a perfect gentleman, and this statement was followed up by a carton of cigarettes each month after.

On the following morning, with most of us sporting monstrous hangovers from the "Fog Lifting," we threw our haversacks over our shoulders and climbed the gangplank onto the ship. I was going for my first cruise across the wide Atlantic.

| 05/30/43 | **Louis Pasteur** | **Atlantic Ocean** | **Crossing the River** |

(Much wider than the St. Lawrence, and we saw submarines everywhere)

A large number of Air Force officers, of whom I was a member, had to be berthed in the main salon, because of a shortage of staterooms. So we were given mattresses, blankets and a piece of the floor to sleep on. But nobody bothered to tell us where the blankets had been before we received them. As it turned out, they had most recently covered Italian POWs making the trip west on the same ship. By the time of arrival in England, little white creatures were crawling all over my body — crabs. I was almost too embarrassed to seek treatment in Bournemouth, but when I did, half the salon-dwellers were in line for blue ointment.

As this was my first sea voyage, it proved a lot to me. Firstly, I had the stomach for a seafaring job, if I wished one. I never missed a meal all the way across, even in rough weather. The others at my table melted away at the first sign of a wave. Had I wished, on rough days, I could have enjoyed seven other meals beside my own. Still my weight was beginning to climb, from 136 pounds at enlistment to 155 today, and I didn't push the free meals.

Although I didn't smoke when I boarded the ship, with cigarettes at 6 cents per pack, I did by the time I got off. This curse I was destined to hold onto for many years after the war. At the time, many of us discarded what we thought were unnecessary items from our luggage, and filled the space with cigarettes and chocolate bars, which also were being sold for a song.

All the way across the Atlantic we searched for submarines. Every 10 minutes somebody spotted one. It seemed totally illogical that a periscope would pop up, every 10 minutes, when your ship is traveling at 29 knots, faster than any U-boat in existence. But we still hung out around the lifeboats, just in case.

Finally, after about five days at sea, we saw the coast of Ireland, with the beautiful fields of green. The Spitfires arrived and circled the ship while we crossed the Irish Sea to our destination, Liverpool. Then I received my first sight of wartime damage; Liverpool was a shambles with bombed out buildings as far as one could see. This was my mother's home, and I dreaded telling her what I saw in my next letter.

Scotland Yard did little to improve our first impressions of Britain. We showered the longshoremen with cigarettes and candy, as a friendly gesture, but the police confiscated everything. Even gifts were frowned on, it would seem. After about a day of waiting, we disembarked from the ship, boarded our waiting train, and proceeded on to our first posting in England. This was Bournemouth, the aircrew collection point on the south coast.

06/06/43   Bournemouth   Reception   #3 Personnel Reception Centre

(My first home in Britain. While it was attractive, it would be a lot nicer place in peacetime)

Most of the Canadian airmen coming to England were sent to Bournemouth prior to any other posting. It gave us a chance to get acquainted with the country, as well as give the authorities an opportunity to sort us out. We did receive some orientation lectures while here, with the most poignant being told how few of us would be making the homeward bound trip. Currently, one in three would not go home.

One of the major problems with Bournemouth was that it was on the south coast; an easy target for intruders. On one sunny Sunday stroll through the central park, we were strafed by three ME-109s that came zooming overhead. We scattered behind park benches, avoiding the bullets, but others were not quite so lucky. This was our first indication that those guys just across the channel were really serious about killing us. We were finally in the war!

The region was a quite historic area, with many famous sites to be seen. The closest was Christchurch, where I and a buddy spent a day around the ancient cathedral. We did not have a lot of time here for travel, but I swore I would come back when I could. However, there was Margaret, who made the stay in town much more pleasant, and a good introduction to the English ladies.

As it would be a few weeks before my next posting, I was given a short leave. I took off north to Southport, where I visited Aunt Francis, my mother's sister, whom I had never met. She had a husband and three young daughters, all in their teens. After a few days of getting acquainted, my careful resolve broke down, and I presented the nylons to the daughters. These had been purchased for other, more nefarious, liaisons; now I would have to depend on my charm, which hadn't really done much for me until then.

Perhaps somebody up there was punishing me for such thoughts, because my next posting was almost to the far ends of the earth.

Notes:

Crabs: *the little white creatures were a very common occurrence for servicemen. They were obtained from many sources, including other people, dirty living conditions and blankets. While quite irritating, they were not otherwise dangerous.*

Chapter 5

THE CREWMEMBER

(70 percent; slow but works hard; should do well with further experience.)

Millom had only two things going for it, the flying and the coal mining. The town itself consisted of row after row of dingy homes, with only the occasional pub thrown in for relief. There were few available young ladies, since most had left town for greener fields. I was able to meet only one, and she was home on leave from the Army Territorial Service.

The air station itself was located with the Irish Sea on one side and miles of dust on the other. The food served was about the worst I had ever encountered in the Air Force; everything came out of one of two pots and was hardly recognizable as food. If it hadn't been for the NAAFI, we might have been tempted to quit eating. I did make a few new friends while there, and one of them was the station Padre. Then the event occurred that changed me from the innocent young lad to the cynic I became later.

One day I was talking to the Padre and he told me he was leaving and going into the hospital. When I asked if it was serious, he said, "Not really. Just a little venereal disease." Men of the cloth just did not catch those things; just we normal people did!

Part of the original crew. Shown from left are Sid Philp, navigator; Neal, bomb-aimer; Jim Hope, WOP-AG; Johnny Loyst, tail gunner; and Chester McClure, pilot. Within months, McClure was in a POW camp, and later, an evader like Neal.

The type of plane I flew at Wellesbourne.

Training at Millom consisted of more cross-countries, with navigation and bombing, and was just another version of Malton, except that the land we flew over was Britain instead of Ontario. We had to be a lot more careful now in that the foe was only a few hundred miles away, not across the ocean. Twin-engine Ansons made easy targets.

When my training was over at Millom, I was sent on another leave, this one for two weeks. I went to London to see what the great capital city was all about. I was impressed by all the famous buildings I had only heard about until then — Parliament, Westminster Abbey, the Tower, St. Paul's, Trafalgar Square, Picadilly Circus, etc. But the best find of all was the Universal Brasserie, a pub located on the Circus. Here I met Margaret Arnold and her sister, both of whom lived in Hammersmith.

Margaret was a lovely lady, and she and her family, became very good friends of mine during my leaves in London. They put me up in their home (I used the son's room; he was with the RAF in North Africa) and we spent many happy evenings at the local pub. I later began to suspect that much of the friendship was designed so that I would take Margaret home to Canada with me. Later on, I found out that my mother was quietly working towards the same end. To Mom, no bride was worth her salt unless she had been born in Britain.

Once my leave was over, I traveled to North Central England for my next posting. Had I only studied more English literature in high school, I would have known that I was now very close to the home of William Shakespeare. But it was time to start crewing up, to find a pilot, a navigator, a wireless operator, an engineer and a couple of air gunners. This was the time to start getting ready for the real flying that was ahead of us!

The first thing they did to us, shortly after arrival at the station, was to throw all the airmen into the same room. We were now expected to get acquainted, and to sort ourselves out into crews of five. Within a few minutes I had met Chester McClure, a pilot from Ottawa. Soon we grabbed Syd Philp, from Montreal, as navigator. Jim Hope, of Toronto, came with us as wireless op, and Johnny Loyst, from Oshawa, as gunner. Evidently a prime bunch of aviators, ready to take on the best the Luftwaffe had to offer. We would pick up the balance of the crew at Conversion Unit.

Then the training started. We had a lot of ground school to cover, but finally our flying was done in something a little more formidable than an Anson. Our training was in Wellingtons, fondly called "Wimpys," that had until recently been flying operations over Europe. Most of them had been well-battered, but they still flew well enough for a bunch of trainees. At first we spent time with flight instructors, but soon Chester soloed, and we were on our way. This was a completely different kind of flying than any of us had done before!

It was something of a miracle that the entire class was not wiped out on these Wimpys. They had seen many hours of rough handling before we ever got to them, both in bombing raids and training. However, we were involved in only one crash landing during our training. One September evening, we were doing circuits and bumps, which meant taking off, circling the field, and landing. On the final landing of the evening, the landing was a little rougher than usual, causing the right undercarriage to fold. The plane swung to the right off the runway, and headed across the field, at full landing speed.

For some unknown reason, I was sitting on the floor, braced against the main spar, rather than beside Chester, which was my normal position. Even better, I was right below the roof escape hatch. We had hardly skidded to a stop before I was out of the plane and running across the field. When I finally stopped, I could hear Chester still calling for me to get out. I guess he did not know that I could run that fast, when my life was at stake. Jim Hope was the only casualty, and he was back with the crew the following day.

The chief Instructor was a typical permanent RAF type, and there was little we could do that would please him. There was little credit for doing things right, but lots of wrath for things done wrong. His saving grace was his love for the bottle; enough booze and he was fair game for any brave student. I took advantage of this, one evening in the mess, by telling him what I thought of him. Fully expecting reprisal the following morning, to my relief none came. We must have both been further gone than I had thought.

Our few trips away from Wellesbourne were mainly to Warwick, about a half-hour by bus. It was impressive to see all of the strange English architecture, after the standard Canadian buildings we had so long been used to. We were also achieving a taste for the English "brews," and the Warwick pubs began to see a lot more of us. I also was finding out that I had crewed up with a group of fellow pub-crawlers.

Chester was a very proficient pilot, soloing in the Wimpy after only a week, but he had a bit of a mean streak in him. He loved to do low flying, regardless of how panic-stricken the rest of the crew might be. Quite often after a cross-country or bombing exercise, he would fly back home at tree-top level. I certainly hoped this was not the way he would fly over Berlin! Finally, by the middle of September, we were all checked out on the two-engine Wellington, and sent on to try our luck on the four-engine Halifax.

10/15/43   **Dalton**   **#2 Battle School**   **Escape and Evasion**

(Completed Course Satisfactorily)

Before we could try out those four-engine jobs, we had to be trained on what to do if we were ever shot down in enemy territory and not captured. It was our duty to work our way back to Allied territory and resume operations. These exercises started as simulated evasions, using the Home Army in place of the German troops we could expect across the channel. The Home Army soldiers were expected to make prisoners of us if caught, but there were some rumors going around that they preferred to take our clothes away and send us off, to get home as best we could. Fortunately, I was never caught, and my modesty never had to stand the test.

We completed three successful evasions, but the fourth and last was just a little too much.

Dropped off on the very remote Yorkshire moors, many miles from home, we debated the point of making the long walk. A passing bus decided the matter, and piling in, we took off for Middlesboro. After a long pub crawl and an overnight stay, we took the morning train back to Dalton. Station personnel were not too pleased by our diversion, and another seven days on base was our reward. But the long walk we had passed up, and the fine party in Middlesboro, made it all worth while.

Mainly this stop was designed not only for escape and evasion, but to hold us until there was space at one of the heavy conversion units. However, six months later, the training that I did go through served me in good stead during the more serious part of my career. After this course was finished, we went on a week's leave to Glasgow, and then on to our next posting.

10/25/43   **Topcliffe**   **#1659 Conversion Unit**   **Halifaxes**

(Capable but a little lazy at times. Good average)

This was our introduction to four-engine bombers, which we would be flying on operations. Joining the crew was Alf Kemp as flight engineer and Frank Minton as mid-upper gunner. We now had the full complement of seven flyers. Topcliffe was probably the best English station I had been on so far. The CO was a Canadian and made special efforts to see that his aircrew trainees received special food. In the two years I was overseas, this was the one and only place I tasted steak.

There was much to learn on the ground about the Halifax, and it was three weeks before we got into the air again. These big fellows were a major change from what we had been flying over the past year and a half. I was now expected to act as copilot, and it was my responsibility to bring the plane back home should anything happen to Chester over Europe. I did get my hours at the controls, but if anybody asked me to land the plane, or take off, they were out of luck.

We trained very hard on these rather ancient bombers (they had already done

Painting of a Halifax bomber like the one the Neal was forced to abandon over Laon in 1944.

24

their share of trips over Europe, and were now consigned to the trembling hands of the trainees), and finally we were ready to go on for our tour of operations. By the end of November, we were posted to Croft in Yorkshire, a station utilized by #6 Group of RAF Bomber Command. We were ready for operations!

12/03/43   Croft   #434 "Bluenose" Squadron   #6 Group of BC

Reality soon took over! Chester was shot down over Mannheim, before the rest of us ever got a chance. He was sent out as a "second dickie" (second pilot with an experienced crew, to give him some familiarization in action) and the plane did not return. We later heard that Chester had been taken prisoner of war, and later that he had escaped and was an evader. It was a big shock to the rest of us, so soon after the end of our training. But it was no surprise to station management, who was seeing two or three planes a night fail to come back. We were the lucky ones.

Perhaps an omen of this loss came a few nights before the Mannheim raid. Doing a long cross-country, over both England and Wales, we ran into problems that almost finished all of us. Above the highlands of Wales, we saw "George," our automatic pilot, go on a rampage, and found ourselves heading straight down. Both Chester and I fought with the control column at length, and finally were able to level off. With the hills up to 4,000 feet and our cruising altitude of 8,000, on a pitch-dark night, there was no way of knowing how much sky was left when we finished.

Later on the same flight, we were struck by lightening. I was in the nose at the time and received a first-class view of it. We were flying through cloud, and a streak of lightening flashed across the sky, and exploded on the nose of the plane. For several seconds we were bathed in a mysterious blue glow. I understood that this was a version of St. Elmo's fire that one hears about in naval stories. While alarming, and potentially lethal, it was a most impressive sight.

With Chester gone, we had to go to another Conversion unit to pick up a new pilot. This time we went to Dishforth, where Eric was waiting for us.

12/28/43   Dishforth   #1664 H.C.U.   2nd Conversion to Halifaxes

Eric Hamber, from Vancouver, BC, joined us as our new pilot. He was a squadron leader when we met him, having spent several years as a pilot in Ferry Command. Now he wanted a tour in Bomber Command. Unfortunately, rank does not always ensure that one is a gentleman!

It was while at Dishforth that I enjoyed my first and only Christmas in England. I accepted an invitation from an English family who lived in Shrewton, near Salisbury. Traveling by train and bus, I arrived the day before Christmas and was given one of their many bedrooms. They were apparently minor aristocracy in the area, and enjoyed a fair-sized manor house.

They were actually a family of three, an elderly grandmother, a younger mother and her teenage daughter. The mother also had two sons, who were currently part of the British Army in North Africa. They also both were full colonels.

I spent several days over the holiday, enjoying their fine hospitality and Christmas dinner. The daughter got out a couple of bikes and we cycled over to Stonehenge, a few miles away. It was most attractive, and certainly not the tourist trap there today. The visit had given me the opportunity to see a British family close up, although they were not your average middle class.

With a few training cross-country flights, we were ready for our tour; over to the "Moose" we were sent. Eric had spent many hours as a pilot of Ferry Command, and did not require a lot of training to handle the Halifax. He was very competent at the controls.

Notes:

Vickers Wellington: *a twin-engine bomber that had been involved in much of the bombing of Europe until then. Nicknamed the "Wimpy," it was being phased out in favor of the four-engine planes, such as the Halifax, the Lancaster and the Stirling.*

Permanent RAF Types: *and, to be fair, RCAF types, were those airmen who had chosen to make a career out of the Air Force before the war, or hoped to after. The rest of us knew that, if we survived, we would be back on Civvie Street once it was over.*

"George": *was the term used for the automatic pilot, but all he normally did was keep us straight and level, while the pilot took a break. Occasionally "George" went on a rampage, and then the crew was in trouble.*

Stonehenge: *I have been back there several times since the war, but it is now far too commercial to be an attractive tourist stop. Sometimes one must consider that improved transportation was one of the negative things that came out of WWII.*

Eric Hamber: *from Vancouver, BC, his uncle had been a lieutenant governor of the province, and had a Provincial park named after him.*

#1 Air Observer School, Malton, Ontario, winter 1942/43. *Trying out the wings the day before Wings Parade. Malton, Ontario 1943.* *Dorothy and I on the Verdun Boardwalk on my embarkation leave 1943.*

Tourists at Christ Church, England. June 1943. *"The Vistors"- Airman from various countires, guests of the Maquis 1944.*

Chapter 6

THE WARRIOR

01/11/44   Middleton St. George   #419 "Moose" Squadron   #6 Group B.C.

Operations at last! Middleton St. George was just about the most northerly of all the stations in Bomber Command, in County Durham, just over the river Tees from Yorkshire. As we reported in, I was assigned to a room on the first floor of the officer's mess, just down the hall from the common lounge. Besides the lounge and the bedrooms, there was a large dining room, the kitchen, and the very necessary pay office.

It was a permanent station, built in prewar days, and had seen many squadrons and airmen, come and go. Now it was the home of #419 "Moose" and #428 "Ghost" Squadrons, both a part of #6 Group of RAF Bomber Command. The group was organized in 1942 in order to give some sort of identity to those members of the RCAF who were flying over Europe on bombing raids. There were some six or seven stations within the group, and about 12 or 14 squadrons, all located in Yorkshire or Durham.

Parked around Middleton St. George were several dozen Halifax bombers, a few of which we would soon be flying over the designated German targets. During the past few months, Bomber Command had concentrated its efforts on the Battle of Berlin, and the station had suffered higher-than-normal losses as a result. It was not very reassuring to hear the other residents of the mess tell us, "Don't get too settled, you won't be here that long!" And they were right; every morning there were more empty places at the breakfast table.

My roommate was the station navigation officer, a squadron leader who had already completed several tours of operations. He was a wild sort of guy, and one of his favorite pastimes included firing his huge pistol out of the window, using telephone poles as targets. He drove a little MG sports car, which he often drove to town using 100 octane aviation gasoline. Quite often, several of us were invited along, and we spent the whole trip hanging on for dear life. With his heavy foot, and the super fuel, it was usually a pretty hairy experience.

A Mark X Avro Lancaster from Neal's squadron. This plane was restored and still is flying today.

Other than this, life on the station proved quite interesting, although at many times it was better described as "wild." When an operation was on, things were normally pretty quiet; we just sat andwaited for the return of our squadron mates. When operations were not on, it was a different matter; a party was the order of the day. While most of these consisted of plenty of drinking, and singing around the piano, there were exceptions. One of these was the night we put on a motorcycle race around the lounge. The chairs were piled up in the centre, and the rest of the floor was the track. I don't remember who won, but we were lucky that no more damage was done than a chair or two. Fortunately for us, some of the top brass was participating in the race.

Many of our nights off were spent in Darlington, a city just a few miles away from the station. I became a quite familiar figure in several places: the Free Mason's Arms, the Cameron Arms, or the King George, all great English pubs. The Free Masons was a great place for music, as they were able to hold on to one of the few bands left in the region. For a real good sing-along, the Free Masons was the place to go.

It was also a place for other, more strange, goings-on. One airman ran out of drinking money and decided that a public auction of his trousers might solve this problem. So he stood on a table and accepted bids. How he would return to base without trousers never occurred to him, or anyone else. The senior lady that ran the place and I became friends, and I was titled "her Little Boy." I spent many happy hours there.

The Cameron Arms did not offer as much music, but it did offer good beer and a place to meet the ladies. The ladies were not always nice, and I did have to use force to stop one not-so-nice lady. She accused me of being "yellow livered" because I would not succumb to her wiles. Her friends agreed that I had applied the necessary force, but it was my one and only woman-beating.

But this was where I met Edna! She was then the barmaid at the pub, and we met by talking across the bar. Her home was in Middlesboro, about half an hour away by train, and she had just recently started this job. Only 18, Edna was a pretty young thing and we quickly became close friends. Within a month, this was developing into pretty serious stuff, especially when she invited me home to meet the folks.

The King George was more of a family pub; a good place for a quiet pint and a good conversation. I met a few strange people here; one was an interesting lady in her 80s. While we talked, she enjoyed her pint of ale and puffed away on her corncob pipe. The English people were certainly different from the people I had known back home.

From the time we arrived at Croft, back in November, until I left Middleton St. George by parachute in April 1944, a lot of my free time was spent going from one of these pubs to the other. Once I met Edna, the Cameron saw most of my attention. Then, when we heard the inevitable call, "Time please, ladies and gentlemen!" it was a mad rush to make the last train home. On many a dark night, when no planes were in the air, happy airmen climbed off the train, and merrily made their way back to barracks.

Edna Tomlinson, the other pretty lady that I lost out on as a result of my adventure in France. Dancing in 1993 with her husband, Barney.

There was, of course, also the Oak Tree, called "The Twig," just off the base, where we could get a beer when we couldn't get to town. Sometimes we had to be reminded that there was a war on, and which had to be won before we could go back home. So, pub crawling became the smaller part of our activities, and getting on with the job became the priority.

Bombing operations with Eric were to prove quite interesting. The first one we did was on the city of Magdeburg, on Jan. 21, 1944. The first 10 days of our stay were used in familiarization, but then our crew was posted for that night. Takeoff was about 7:30 p.m. and the inward flight was done between solid layers of cloud. Except for one short break, we were almost totally unable to see the sky or the ground. But, by the most fortunate of chances, the one break allowed me to take a star shot of Polaris, the North Star. Right after the clouds closed in again. But this one shot was just enough to get us over the target, and almost on time.

The target was afire, making a good aiming point for us, and I dropped my bombs right into the target indicators that the Pathfinders had laid out for us. After closing the bomb doors, we turned away from the city, and headed north towards the North Sea. That is when the good times ended!

A few minutes out of the target area, we ran into an antiaircraft barrage; what ever they used, they certainly had our range. Round after round exploded close to the airplane, and much of the shrapnel found us. I had just checked my bomb bays, then froze while the barrage went on. Right after, I looked behind me, and there was a hole in the fuselage, about 6 to 8 inches in diameter, inches from my head.

Then the searchlights found us; we were caught by one and about a dozen others honed in on us right after. It was the strangest feeling; to be like a little fly in the night, with everybody's flashlight pointed at us. Eric threw that airplane all over the sky in an effort to throw off the lights. Eventually he was successful in this, but by this time the night fighters had found us. We were attacked three times, but each time we corkscrewed to get away from them, and were never fired upon. In fact, during the final attack, Johnny Loyst fired back, and was able to claim one fighter as shot down. We made it the rest of the way back home without further incident.

Through all of this, nobody in the crew was wounded, although we had taken a lot of flak. But I knew we had a heck of a pilot, and a sure-shot of a gunner. We were diverted to Lakenheath, a RAF base in East Anglia, and spent the night there. The following morning, we counted over 100 holes in the plane and were told it was a write-off. We had to wait until another Halifax came to pick us up before we could go back to Middleton St. George. In spite of the damage, the operation was considered a success.

The second trip, a week later, was to Berlin, and in some ways, even hairier than the first. Take-off was at 10 minutes after midnight, and getting to the target was again no problem. We saw no enemy fighters, were not bothered much by flak, and bombed accurately on the target indicators. But coming out north from the target was where the problems began. The winds were blowing at about 120 mph, and with our airspeed about 165, we were almost standing still; good targets for just about anybody. We survived several attacks, one of them being from another British bomber, without damage. However, while Eric was tossing the plane around, I also was being tossed around, and receiving a banged-up leg in the process. After what seemed hours, we finally reached Denmark, where we turned west towards England and home.

But we were not yet finished with perils we would face that night! We crossed the North Sea, just above the clouds, and as daylight began to show, were treated to the most beautiful sight of a sunrise above a fleecy horizon. Little did we realize that these same clouds would almost prove our downfall.

As was very normal for this time of year, Middleton St. George was fogged in; we were diverted to Coltishall, a fighter base in East Anglia. Coltishall control reported a low ceiling and asked us to let down over the sea. We complied, and after many minutes of letting down in cloud, finally broke free; within a foot or two of the water. I was Eric's eyes in the nose, and I yelled for him to pull up. He got us back into the clouds, but I am convinced, even today, that we bounced off the North Sea. Of course, when we later let down over Coltishall, we found the 400 feet of ceiling they had somehow forgotten about. A few hours after landing, the weather cleared, and we returned home.

Our third trip was again to Berlin, on Feb. 15 — rotten weather had kept us on the ground for two weeks — but this time the resistance came from another quarter. We flew across Germany without seeing any fighters or flak, but about 50 miles before the target, Eric ordered me to drop the bombs. He apparently did not want to continue across Berlin, but wanted to turn back early. I could not understand this, since previous bombings had been right on target, and I did not want to bring the bombs all this way to drop on open fields. So, in one of the few obstinate deeds of my career, I refused to follow the order, and forced him on to the target before I would release the bombs.

Once this happened, our third trip was another successful one, as my bombs went dead-on to the target. But this did not seem to please Eric, as he and I were no longer on speaking terms. He did not seem to like being disobeyed, and I had refused to accept his order. Thus began a parting of the ways, although this did not come about for another month.

Again we were diverted, this time to Bury St. Edmonds, out of which the U.S. Air Force were flying B-17 Fortress bombers. We stayed there for three whole days while the weather cleared over our home base. All the time we enjoyed those little pleasures we had not seen since Canada: ice cream, fresh eggs, steaks and North American beer. What was really amazing was the amount of money changing hands during the ever-ongoing poker games. We were obviously grossly underpaid for doing the same jobs, and taking the same risks, as these guys. But, of course, we were doing it for the glory.

The fourth and fifth trips were less than ideal. One was a recall and the other a spoof (to pull the German fighters up, while the main bomber force went elsewhere). Our sixth operation was to Kiel, where we laid a number of aerial mines in the harbour. The seventh was another mining operation to Brest in Brittany. When I was not quite certain of my aiming point, I forced Eric to do a circuit so I would have another shot at the harbour. There was no point in coming all this way and dumping the mines in the wrong place. While there was little enemy opposition, I am certain this did not endear me to Eric.

The eighth was to Trappes, just south of Paris, where we bombed the Renault tank factory. This was about the most successful operation so far and I received the target photo award for putting my bombs closer to the target than anyone on the squadron. However, the next was our last as a crew, and was to Le Mans in northwest France. The target was covered by 10/10 cloud and, after circling for an hour, we brought our bombs back to England. While landing, Eric was very verbally abusive, and I protested in rather strong terms. I didn't think four-letter words were really necessary.

The following day, he called a crew meeting during which I voiced my concern about our continued cooperation as a crew. I was getting along well enough with the rest of the fellows, but Eric was the major problem. I decided to resign from the crew and go on the spare list until I could find another crew. It had all been a matter of too many four-letter words, and too much interference in my bombing responsibilities.

All this time Edna and I were becoming a close twosome, and I was close to proposing to her. Before this could happen, she quit her job at the Cameron Arms, and enlisted in the Women's Division of the RAF. Sadly, I saw her off on the train for her basic training, and my proposal was deferred. To ease my disappointment on the break-up of my crew, I was sent on a 14-day leave, and went to Southport to see Aunt Francis once more. Stayed with them a week, and with my ration coupons, they were able to serve roast beef for one of the rare occasions of the war. And with my Uncle, played the only game of gold I was able to get in while in Britain.

The second week was spent in the region; downtown Southport offered a lot of carousing that could not be passed up. Hooked up with a couple of British sailors on shore leave, and we tore the town apart. There were plenty of lovely ladies to go around. But too soon the time came for return to base, and the sailors drove me to the train station in Liverpool, where they were rejoining their ship. I took the train and was back at Middleton St. George in a few hours.

Shortly after my return, I spared for the crew piloted by a Pilot Officer Edwards, members of 428 Squadron. Their bomb-aimer was in the hospital. The pilot was a lot different from Eric, and a real gentleman when it came to other members of his crew. Given the chance to do my own thing, the next two trips were the most successful of my tour. On April 9, we went to Lille, France, and on April 10 to Ghent, Belgium. In both cases, marshalling yards were the target, and plenty of explosions noted in both cases. Some of the smoke came up almost to our level.

At the same time, I had been getting to know a crew that was having medical problems with their bomb-aimer. Eventually I was asked to join them, since it was unlikely their other member would be back. Unfortunately, it was not to be — or fortunately, as the case may be. Later in the year, that crew went out on a daylight raid over Germany and never returned. Other crews reported that the plane blew up, and no parachutes were seen. I would have been with them.

Shortly after the two raids with P/O Edwards, I went on a few days' leave so that I could visit Edna. She was still doing her "square bashing" but we managed a few hours for a walk. On the walk, I proposed and was accepted. I returned to base on Cloud Nine. But somebody else had no future for our romance, so it seemed.

On April 22, I filled in for the bomb-aimer of the crew piloted by Lt. Chuck Thomas, also of 419 Squadron. This was their first operation, having arrived on base about the time I went to visit Edna. The target was the Laon marshalling yards, in northeast France, about two hours away — fast in and fast out! At this phase of the war, this would normally have been a milk run. But on that night, we were the target, instead of the railway yards.

So, around 11:30 p.m., we found ourselves floating down to earth over France, instead of returning safely home. This was the start of a great new adventure in my Air Force career, and the start of a whole new story.

Notes:

B.C.: *Bomber Command*

Middleton St George: *today known as Teeside Airport. The officer's mess, where I lived, is the St. George's Hotel.*

Operations: *each trip a crew made over enemy territory was termed an "operation"; 30 operations constituted a tour in Bomber Command, and usually 20 for the second tour.*

(i) You remember Bloody Mary? *"With 'er 'ead tucked underneath 'er arm" — that was how I could have arrived back at base.*

(ii) Lakenheath: *an RAF bomber base that operated with Stirlings. Contrary to Middleton St. George, it was in a dry and dusty location. It is still an active Air Force station today.*

THE CATERPILLAR

Bombyx Mori! Such an unusual, and prophetic, title for a very ancient creature. The Silkworm, discovered many thousands of years ago, was responsible for saving many lives during the World War II.

Silk, one of the strongest of all fibres, was chosen to serve in the earliest parachutes. The first actual use of a parachute was in 1783 by French physicist Sebastien Lenormand. It had been well developed by the time of WWI, but was not often used during combat flying in that conflict.

However, during WWII, all flyers on the Allied side, and many on the Axis side, carried parachutes. This device saved countless lives on both sides.

By the time of this war, nylon had begun to replace silk as the main fabric of the parachute. However, just after the First Great war, Leslie Irving of the Irving Parachute Co., remembering the little creature who started it all, introduced the Caterpillar Club. The only eligible members were those persons who had, in order to save their lives, jumped from a plane (or other flying object) by parachute.

Ever afterwards, these members were entitled to wear the small gold Caterpillar with the ruby eyes as a symbol of their accomplishment. And, to call themselves "Caterpillars".

This is the story of one such Caterpillar, and what happened to him after he had "hit the silk."

Chapter 7

OUT OF THE SKY

The first time I met the new crew was at briefing; they had only arrived on the base about the time I left to see Edna. Their bomb-aimer was in the hospital with jaundice, and I was asked to take his place, at least for this trip. Besides Chuck Thomas, the pilot, there was Bob Lindsay, the navigator, Pat Murphy, the wireless operator, John Thompson, the engineer, Arnold Greene, the mid-upper gunner and Vic Knox, the tail gunner. This was their first operation.

The target was the marshalling yards at Laon in northeast France; this gave me a sense of relief as it would normally be a "milk run" trip. Two hours to reach the target, and another two hours to return home; we should hardly work up a sweat. I did my best to reassure my nervous crewmates, but little did I know that our logbook entries would be made by someone else that night.

With briefing over, we managed dinner and a few necessary chores before heading out to the dispersal area where Halifax J was waiting for us. Everything was ready, bombs, fuel and ammunition all on board, and just waiting for a crew. After a short wait, we did the traditional relief job on the tail wheel, and climbed aboard. Chuck started the engines and taxied out to join the marshalling line-up. By 8:30, we were climbing up into the darkening sky.

We headed south over England, crossed beachy Head, the English Channel, and then the French coast. There was no sign of resistance from either the German fighters or the anti-aircraft guns, making it look as if the milk run was our future. Then Chuck turned south east and I went into the nose to get the bombs ready for the drop — didn't want any foul-ups over the target, had already had enough circuits over the target with Eric. Then I went into the astrohatch to watch for enemy fighters.

A listing of crew members over Laon the night Neal's plane went down. The crew ahead of theirs included Andrew Mynarski, who was awarded a posthumous Victoria Cross several weeks later.

About half-hour later, I went once again into the nose; it was time for the attack. Chuck turned due east towards the target, I put the bombs on live, set up my bombsight, and opened the bomb doors. We had barely seconds before "bombs away" would be called, and we would be headed for home. We did not get those seconds!

I could see the target indicators right below us, well lit-up, and with no clouds in the sky, conditions seemed ideal for direct hits on the rail yards. I followed the target down the bombsight until it was almost at the cross-hairs, and I was holding the release button, ready to press it. Just at that moment came the "big bang"!

A strange voice echoed through the intercom, "What's that?" A loud "thunk" occurred at that point, which made me stop my action with the release button. A vivid flash of light illuminated the entire plane, and more loud thunks echoed through the fuselage behind me. It was a certainty that we had been hit, but just how badly I could not tell at this point. When I tried to call Chuck, I found the intercom had been knocked out. We were also turning sharply north and there was no way I could resume my bomb run at the moment.

Dropping the release, I checked over my body for wounds and finding none, rushed into the cockpit to see what had happened to us. Sure enough, both port engines and part of the fuselage were on fire. We had been caught by a night fighter, and evidently without us seeing him first. I could see that Chuck had been wounded but still was able to handle the plane. He was struggling to get away from the target area and level off. All he could say to me as I stood there was, "Get the hell out." I took this for the bail-out order, and turned back to my nose position for my parachute.

Suddenly remembering all those live high-explosive bombs still on board, I shouted back to Chuck, "Hold everybody a minute. Let me get the bombs away first." Going into the nose, I set all the bombs on safe and pushed the jettison button. I felt the bombs leave, and heaved a sigh of relief. But this did not last long, as I strapped on my chest parachute and turned to the nose escape hatch. Bob Lindsay joined me, and together we kicked the door out into the night. Right away Bob jumped through.

Then it was my turn. I sat down on the edge of the hatch ready to go. The last person I saw was Pat Murphy, blood streaming down his face, and yelling, "Get out, get out." I pushed outward and let go. Then I found that I had pushed too hard; I hit the other side

My soft piece of landing earth north of Laon.

of the hatch first, then slid straight down. As a result, my chin hit the edge as I was pulled out into the night, and I suffered a sore chin for weeks after.

But at least I was alive; I pulled the ripcord right after departure and in seconds I had a fully-opened canopy above me. Now I was heading for the ground, 6,000 feet below us, and to an unknown future. I had never had any training in bailing out, having to make do with verbal instructions. Thank goodness there was something that I could do without a lot of training! But now, all I could see while hanging from the shroud lines, was one plane on fire, and moving rapidly away from me.

However, the fire was probably not yet big enough for the Luftwaffe pilot. Seeking to make certain of his "kill," he flew on after Halifax J, passing a few yards above my shroud. This caused some severe swaying, which took me all over the sky and scared the "H" out of me. It took several minutes before the swaying stopped, and I was once more heading for the ground. Then the next hazard cropped up.

Having bailed out very close to the target, I received an excellent show of the fireworks going on. But then somebody in the bomber stream hit an ammunition train, and up towards me came everything on board. It is quite difficult to reduce one's self in size, while in a parachute, but what I did must have succeeded; everything went whizzing on by. I was glad the sky was a big place!

Then I hit the ground. From 6,000 feet I should have known it wouldn't take long, but I wasn't ready for it; the fireworks were too interesting. Besides, on such a dark night, there was no way I could see the ground, or where I was coming down to. Fortunately the French farmers had just completed their plowing, and my touchdown was right in the centre of one of their fields. A few stars showed up, but they soon disappeared, and I was safely on the ground. I collected my parachute and sat down for a while to consider my situation. The shrapnel was still flying around, and I had to stay out of the line of fire.

Finally the raid came to an end, and the survivors headed for home. Now I was able to do some thinking; I was a stranger in a strange land, and had no immediate idea of what to do. We were supposed to try for escape and rejoin our units if possible. The suggested route was towards Paris, where more Resistance people were operating, but to try for help along the way. So I checked my button compass, and prepared to set out in a southwest direction. But again I had to delay this!

The voices started up close by; it was hard to tell what language they were speaking, what they were doing, or even what sex they were. Another half-hour passed before they faded away, and my departure was clear. They were probably French, since I would have been easy to find had they been German searchers. They could not have been more than 20 or 30 feet away. Could have been an amorous liaison, but certainly I wouldn't have been as quick as they were!

Then I got ready, and took off southwest towards the "City of Lights." This took a little longer to achieve than I had expected, because of the side trips I was forced to take along the way.

Notes:

On arrival back in England, I was told that Chuck had escaped through Spain, and was already back in Florida in a veteran's hospital. Some fast escape!

Sgt. Filipzig: *pilot of a ME-110, from Unit NJG-1 of the Luftwaffe, was reported to have shot down our plane (from J. Hallade, in "La Guerre Aerienne et la Liberation de*

L'Aisne"). We were his first kill, which seemed rather ironic since most of us were on our first trip, one of us for the second time.

6,000 feet: *our bombing height. Some members of the crew reported dropping to 2,000 feet by the time of bailout, but I don't remember any sudden dives.*

Button compass: *I wore a compass built into one of the buttons on my battledress jacket.*

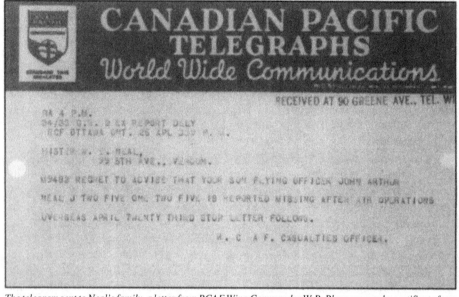

The telegram sent to Neal's family, a letter from RCAF Wing Commander W.P. Pleasance and a certificate from the Canadian Minister of National Defence for Air announcing Neal's missing-in-action status.

To Mr. and Mrs. William Edward Neal
I have learned with deep regret
that Flying Officer John Arthur Neal, R.C.A.F.
has been reported missing.
The Government and people of Canada join
me in expressing the hope that more favourable news
will be forthcoming in the near future.

Minister of National Defence for Air

IN REPLY PLEASE QUOTE

FILE No. 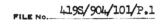 419S/904/101/P.1

ROYAL CANADIAN AIR FORCE
OVERSEAS

No. 419 (R.C.A.F.) Squadron,
"MOOSE SQUADRON"

28th April, 1944.

Dear Mrs. Neal:

I regret having to confirm the telegram, which you have already received, notifying you that your son, Flying Officer John Arthur Neal, is missing from operations on the night of April 22nd, 1944. The mission from which he failed to return was an attack on an important objective in enemy occupied territory but, unfortunately, nothing has been heard of the aircraft or crew since take-off. There is still quite a possibility that all or part of the crew may be safe or prisoners of war but news of this could not be expected for some considerable time yet.

Your son was with us for $3\frac{1}{2}$ months and had successfully completed ten operations against the enemy. He seemed to be a very happy lad who was quite content in his duties as a Bomb Aimer and, as a result, became quite popular with the remainder of the lads of the Squadron.

If any further news comes to hand, you may rest assured you will be notified immediately.

F/O Neal's kit and personal effects have been collected and forwarded to the Central Depository, Colnbrook, Slough, Bucks., who, after completion of necessary details, will communicate with you as to their disposal.

May I convey my sincere sympathy to you in your great loss, and hope with you that better news may follow.

Yours sincerely,

(W.P. Pleasance) Wing Commander,
Commanding 419 (RCAF) Squadron.

Mrs. W.E. Neal,
99 5th Avenue,
Verdun, P.Q. Canada.

Chapter 8

WALKING TO PARIS

My first chore, before I could leave, was to get rid of my parachute, harness and Mae West. I dug a shallow pit in the plowed field and buried the first two. They would be easy to find by daylight but I hoped to be many miles away by that time. With the compass in my hand, I started out southwest; after about a mile I came to a copse of trees where I deposited the Mae West. Thus unencumbered, I continued on in the direction that I hoped would eventually take me to the Resistance forces.

After a short distance, I came on a burning plane; quite possibly Halifax J, although I did not think it would have come down this close to the target. It was still too dark to see what type of plane it was. As I started to walk around it, the ammunition in the plane began to detonate. Once again I dropped to the ground, not wanting to come all this way just to get killed by my own plane! Finally it ran out of bullets, and I got up and continued my walk.

I had not seen anything of the other crewmembers until now and could only assume they had all gotten out of the plane. It was pretty hard to see anything on a night as dark as this one was. While musing about the other crewmembers, I failed to notice the trip wire lying across my path. Stumbling over it, I fell into the brush through which I was walking at the time. It was evidently an alarm system of some kind. Picking myself up, I waited for a few moments to see if I had raised any hue and cry. When none came, I carried on and shortly broke out onto a large, flat, grassy area. I kept walking across this field, still in a southwesterly direction.

It was still quite dark and I could see nothing, not even the grass I was walking on. Then, suddenly, the grass turned to pavement, and a few minutes later, back to grass. Suddenly, there was a huge roar close by, and an airplane swooped off the ground right beside me. I was in the middle of an airport, of all the bloody stupid places to be! The tripwire must have been their warning system. The Germans probably hadn't heard me since many of them were occupied with shooting us down. Either that, or they were goofing off, just as we did part of the time.

Thus warned, I ran the rest of the way across the field until I reached the perimeter path. Passing a couple of small buildings there, I had the silly idea they might offer sanctuary from my potential searchers. Entering one of them, I soon found out its normal use, and abandoned it in a hurry. The strong and not too pleasant aroma did prove out one old rumor; the Germans consume a lot of cabbage. I would have to look elsewhere for a haven.

I continued into the woods that bordered the far side of the airport and was successful this time in avoiding any tripwires. After walking what seemed many miles, the first signs of the coming of dawn began to show on the horizon. It was time for me to start seeking true sanctuary for the daylight hours. I was by now determined to avoid capture and to reach Paris, if it was humanly possible. With the light growing still stronger, I spotted a large haystack in the middle of the field that I was then crossing. From our days of escape training, these were the recommended hiding places when on the run. Drawing near, I saw a large tunnel running completely through the stack, just a few feet above the ground. Gathering several bales from the stack, I covered both entrances, climbed inside, and went to sleep.

A few hours later, I was awakened by the sound of many voices. Peeking out, I saw a small army of workers busy working the soil of the field. Around them were a half dozen or so German soldiers, obviously standing guard over the workers. I had hidden right in the middle of a work party! I could see that it was going to be a very long, quiet, day.

When lunch time rolled around, several of the workers strolled over to my haystack to eat. They sat just outside my tunnel, eating away and talking in a language I could scarcely understand at the time. Feeling that I really had little to lose, and since the guards were on the other side of the field, I made my presence known to the workers. Once the initial surprise was over, they gathered up some of their food and gave it to me. Then they warned me about the guards, gave me directions for that night, made my tunnel entrance more secure, and went back to work. All day long I stayed in the tunnel; with no noise, no smoking and no more sleep.

With the arrival of dark, and the workers gone home, I took off again, also southwesterly. Following the directions of the workers, I crossed some railroad tracks and on into the woods that bordered the field. I encountered no major problems through this night; everybody must have been asleep for miles around. I came to the village of Crepy and walked straight through it without being challenged. In the middle of the town was the village fountain; I stopped and filled up the water bottle that had come with the escape kit, and added a water purification pill. At least now I had something to drink.

It was now about 3 a.m. and there was not one person about. Just out of the town, I left the road and kept walking across the fields for another two or three hours, until dawn broke once again, my second in France. It was time to look for another hiding place.

My choice was again a haystack, standing about a half-mile off the road that ran alongside my walking route. This stack did not have a tunnel, but it did have a terrace on top. The terrace was surrounded by a two foot wall made up of bales of hay; when lying on the hay, I could not be seen from anywhere in the surrounding region. There was a house nearby, but it seemed to be adandoned. Just as dawn was fully with me, I snuggled into the hay and went to sleep.

This time there were no workers or Germans to awaken me; it was the sun that did the damage. For late April, Northern France was proving a pretty warm region. Back home we would probably still have snow in many of the fields and ditches, but not here. Wearing my winter blue battledress, by midday I was sweltering from the steady rays of the sun. There was some activity along the nearby roadway, and I even noted a few troops of German soldiers marching along.

Fortunately, none of the passersby gave a thought to my hiding place for that day. Perhaps I was getting more experienced in the tactics of evasion, but I knew it would take many more days like this one to escape successfully from France.

When nighttime again fell, I started out walking towards the heavy woods that I could see just beyond the farm. I was getting a little more brave now; my route would be along the road I had watched for most of the day. Fortunately, the region again seemed deserted; there must have been some kind of curfew on, once dark fell.

By this time, I was also getting very hungry. I had very little to eat in the past two days, save the donations of the field workers, and the Horlick tablets in my escape kit. My stomach was growling and I knew I would have to look for a good meal pretty soon. As I was passing two small cottages along the road, I decided I would have to take a chance. Turning in, I rapped on one of the doors; a Lady answered the door. There were several small children crowding around her.

Because I probably presented a rather weird sight, after two days on the road without bathroom facilities, and a nondescript blue uniform, the lady showed a lot of concern at first. Trying to force a smile, I said, in my best high-school French, "Je suis aviateur

Canadien." With that opening, the lady broke into a smile, and waved me into her house. She sent one of her daughters next door to bring their friends over, and before I knew it, I was surrounded by a small crowd of happy, and very friendly, people. Here was the Liberator, at their very door!

The lady broke out a bottle of wine and we had drinks all round. I knew enough of the French to see that they were not locals. After some probing, I learned the truth about these two families; they were from Poland, having escaped when the Germans overran them in 1939. A year later, they were overrun again during the invasion of France. Their men had been taken away as slave labor for German industry. The rest of the families were just trying to survive until the day the men returned.

After the wine, I sat down to a meal that was about as large as their meager supplies would allow. The way they were dressed indicated that these people were having a struggle, not only to eat, but just to stay alive. But they could still find enough food to feed me! My first major contact with people showed what hardships were being endured by the population of German-occupied Europe. I no longer felt quite so lonely as I had before the visit.

When I was ready to leave, the lady of the house packed up some food for me to take along. After some warm good-byes, I walked away and into the woods, that were almost surrounding us at this point. Again I stuck to the road, figuring if anybody came along, I could duck into the trees or the ditch until they were past. Several people and vehicles did come along, but I was well-hidden at the time. The night was again very dark, and a heavy mist was beginning to settle in, making it even harder to see anything around me.

About an hour into my walk, I began to sense that the lady, in all her kindness, had given me a food item that I had not quite gotten used to — Limburger cheese. The pungent aroma of this product began to permeate the air around me. Fearing that this, more than anything else, would give away my location, I was forced to consign the Limburger to the forest. Perhaps it would cause anyone following me to go off on a "false scent."

The mist became even thicker as I progressed through the woods. With the road winding its way among the trees, there was no way I could know how far I would have to go before breaking free. It was just like walking down a long, dark, tunnel. Finally the dark turned to a version of gray, and I knew that dawn was approaching again. Would I be able to find another haystack as my haven for the coming day?

Just as I was beginning to get really worried about this, a small break in the mist revealed two haystacks near the road. I was at a break in the forest, with just enough area for a few small farms to be established. As I approached these two stacks, I saw that one was on each side of the road. Making a rather "eenie-meenie" type of choice, I picked the haystack on the right side of the road. Climbing up on top, I settled into the hay and went to sleep. My third night, and hopefully I would make it through the day undiscovered.

Notes:

In his report, Arnold Greene reported a JU-88 night fighter shot down by Vic Knox. Maybe this was the plane I passed. From where I was in the nose, there was no way I could confirm or deny this.

The airport I crossed was the Laon-Couvron Airport, which probably housed the night fighter that shot us down. It is still an operational station today.

The Germans conscripted all healthy French males, and many females, for work in either German factories or in the fields. The ones I saw were obviously those who were unable to escape the round-ups.

The forest I passed through was the Foret de St. Gobain, which played such a prominent part as a battleground in WWI.

Chapter 9

THE DISCOVERY

Morning broke, and so did my rather vague plans for getting to Paris! The thing that woke me was the barking of a dog. He was at the bottom of my stack, trying valiantly to climb up it to where I was hiding. Although he was unable to make it, his owner had more success. With his pitchfork in hand, he topped the hay, and stared at me. Lying there, almost covered in hay, I stared back. "Je suis aviateur Canadien," I blurted out, still in my best homemade French. Then he grinned, and we talked, in broken French and broken English, for several minutes. I found out he was Mr. Albert Potelle, who owned the haystack I was on, and the house and barn just a few yards away. I did not see these other structures earlier, because of the mist I was in.

He suggested that I stay where I was for the day, and he would bring me into the house after dark. Then he told me, in his completely understandable French, that I had made the most fortunate of choices in my haystacks. The one on the other side of the road, and which had lost out in my "eenie-meenie," belonged to a collaborator. He had already turned three Allied aviators in to the Germans. This had been a very close call, but my good fortune was still holding out. Mr. Potelle brought me some food at noon hour, and I spent the balance of the day admiring the countryside.

Finally it was dark, and I slid down from the haystack and walked with Mr. Potelle into the house. Here I met the rest of the family; Mrs. Potelle, their young daughter, Germaine, and a young nephew. I immediately was made to feel at home. A lot more wine was brought out, and we made plenty of toasts, to everybody and everything we could think of. Then I was treated to just about the best home-cooked meal I had tasted since leaving Canada.

It was all great food, although probably a lot simpler than anything found in a major restauarant. There was potato and leek soup, harricot (bean) salad, roast beef and the trimmings, and of course, wine. There was plenty of everything to fill up my empty belly.

Shown from left are French citizens who helped Neal in his first hiding place: Raymond Tachon, Germaine Potelle's husband; her brother; Germaine Potelle Tachon; her sister-in-law. Potelle's brother had supplied Neal's clothes during this period.

Germaine Potelle and her cousin. The cousin was killed years later during the Algerian War of Independence.

What a contrast to those unfortunate people living just on the other side of the forest! Although it would never have occurred to me at the time, this was the start of my great weight zoom, from 155 lbs. at bailout to 180 lbs. at liberation.

After dinner, Mr. Potelle and I talked about the future. I could not stay around his farm for too long; there were just too many visitors and too many Germans passing by along the road. However, he did have connections with the French Resistance and would call them in to take me into one of their escape lines. This would take a few weeks to set up, but in the meantime I could stay with them. I would sleep in the barn at night, and have the run of the house by day. After a week of sleeping in the barn, and making intimate friends with a family of fleas, they found a bed for me in the house. Thankfully, the fleas and I parted company.

A few days after moving into the house, several strangers arrived to visit with me. They asked me many questions, which I answered, apparently to their satisfaction. Just before leaving, they gave me a parcel of civilian clothing to put on. Included was a beret, a shirt, a sports jacket, trousers and a pair of patent leather shoes, all of which I wore from then on. I was now officially "un Francais," but it would be several weeks yet before I knew my full identity. Also many more weeks before everything would fit perfectly — the donor must have been some big guy; little did I know then that he was Germaine's older brother. Life resumed at the Potelle's, but they were no longer hiding an airman, but a civilian. My uniform, pistol and dog tags were hidden away where it was hoped nobody could find them.

My stay here lasted until May 12. It was a very peaceful stay, except for the one occasion when an elderly German soldier came visiting. He entered the house and caught me while I was talking to Germaine. Fortunately, he was a regular visitor who came to buy eggs and milk. I was cautioned to remain quiet, and shortly after, he left.

Neal's false identity card, making him "Louis Vachere."

French monetary scrip from the Resistance.

As it turned out, he was just a homesick German farmer who couldn't wait for the war to be over so he could go back home. Many members of the German Army, in the rural areas such as this, were similar to this individual.

The postman dropped in almost every day, and we became friends. I didn't really want to leave here, since I was eating so well. Germaine, just a little younger than I, was proving very interesting to a lonely, red-blooded, guy from Canada. Still it had to end sometime. On May 12, the same two men, in a strange, three-wheeled vehicle, arrived to take me away. One of them turned out to be Etienne Dromas, chief of the Resistance forces in the Chauny region where I now was. As a soldier, he had lost a leg during the German invasion of France, and was now getting around quite well on a wooden one. After an emotional farewell with the Potelles, we started back along the same road on which I had arrived.

While we drove through the country, Etienne turned around to me, in the single back seat, and handed over a card. Looking at it, I found it was my new identity card, and I was now Louis Vachere of Bucy le Long. My photo had been included with my escape kit, and it was now pasted on my card, and stamped. Nervously, I signed the name given to me, and was now, officially, a French citizen. Of course this was only valid if it passed scrutiny when, or if, I was ever stopped by the authorities.

We saw very little other traffic on the road, so these guys obviously knew how to get about the region without detection. After close to an hour of driving, we arrived in the village of

Jean Hallade, one of Neal's questioners at Bichancourt the day he met Bob Lindsay. At right is Hallade's son, Pierre.

Bichancourt, located very close to the Oise river, and a few miles away from Chauny.

We pulled up to a house about in the middle of the town, and were ushered inside. Waiting at the door for us were a husband and wife, the owners of the residence. Both were teachers at the local school but had no children of their own. They were to be my host and hostess for about a week, until other arrangements could be made for me. After introductions were made, they showed me to my room on the second floor.

Unknown to me, this stay was also a test; the Resistance had to be absolutely certain that I was a true Allied Airman There were a number of German infiltrators in the region, posing as airmen, who possessed good English accents. More than one Resistance cell had been broken up by the penetration of these agents, and many good French patriots slaughtered.

On the evening of my arrival, a number of visitors arrived at our door. Among them was Bob Lindsay, the navigator from our plane. The others were local Resistance members. Bob and I shook hands and compared notes on our activities up until then. The fact that Bob and I knew one another was enough to convince the Resistance that we were bonafide airmen, and not agents from Berlin. Had they been unsure, we could have readily been disposed of.

After the visitors had departed, I settled in for the balance of the week. As school teachers, the couple were away almost all day, leaving me to my own devices. I had the run of the house from early morning until sundown. They left out the food I would need for my lunch. One day I was left a loaf of French bread. At noon, I broke the loaf open preparing to make myself a sandwich. To my amazement, I found thousands of little black ants crawling around inside the loaf. Not yet having acquired a taste for this type of fare, I quietly returned the loaf to the pantry.

At supper that night, when I described what I had encountered to the couple, they merely smiled, got out the loaf, knocked it against the door jamb, and ate it; ants and all! I certainly still had much to learn about this country.

Notes:

The Potelle house was the last one on the south end of the village of Suzy. I never saw this village until 1987 when I visited Germaine at the farm. Her parents had long since passed away.

I have long searched for a soup similar to the one made by Mrs. Potelle. Only at Chez Bardet's, in Montreal North, have I been able to find it.

I arrived back in England weighing 180 lbs.; if any proof of this is required, I can still show it to the person requesting.

The original Louis Vachere was apparently killed fighting the German invaders in 1940. I was not too enchanted when I translated the name; it was "Louis the Cow."

Etienne Dromas, the leader of the Resistance Forces in the Chauny region, died in January 1996, at the age of 84. He was still proud of his wooden leg, and as late as 1994, we still shared a glass of champagne during my infrequent visits to Chauny.

Chapter 10

THE TOWN OF CHAUNY

At the end of my week in Bichancourt, Etienne Dromas again showed up, and away we drove in his little three-wheeled car. This time we drove into the town of Chauny, just a few miles away from Bichancourt. We crossed the canal, drove by the Chauny railway station, and through the market square. Finally we pulled up at a three-story house, on a narrow little street, right in the centre of town. This was my first real sight of urban French life, and I was quite impressed. The people and the architecture were certainly different from what I had known back home in Canada.

Located at No. 3 Rue General Leclerc, the house was owned by Mr. Louis Daubercies and his wife, a couple who were somewhere in their late 50s. Etienne advised me that this was to be my home until they could arrange my transportation back to England by submarine. Then he departed and I started to get acquainted with my newest host and hostess.

Numbers 3 and 5 Rue General Leclerc, in the middle of the block. The room where Neal stayed is marked with an X.

Mr. Daubercies was a lawyer, and presently the Justice of the Peace for the Chauny region. His family was considered part of the "aristocracy" of the town, and the quality of their life was shown in the beauty of their home. Mrs. Daubercies was an excellent cook and what she could do with a few greens, tomatoes, shallots, and a bit of oil was really mouth-watering. What made this even more remarkable was the scarcity of food supplies available in the town. The Germans were taking away everything worthwhile, and leaving very little for the French themselves. Fortunately, the Daubercies had country connections where they could maintain much of their food supply.

They made me feel very welcome in their home and the first act was to escort me to the second floor where I would be sleeping. Overlooking the street, this was one of the most comfortable-looking bedrooms that I had ever seen. The room belonged to their son, Pierre, who was away studying the law at the Sorbonne in Paris. With their welcome, and the use of the bedroom, I really felt that I was home.

Josette Ponchaux in 1944.

Mrs. Daubercies at the front door of No. 3 Rue General Leclerc.

In comparing the Daubercies with others I had met so far, the French they spoke was so clear that even I, with only my high school lessons, easily could understand them. It was at their home that I really began to speak in the French language, with fewer and fewer problems. But then, besides the Daubercies, I had the best of tutors to help in my lessons.

On the first evening of my stay, we had several visitors from next door. These visitors consisted of Mr. and Mrs. Ponchaux, and their two young daughters, Josette and Mireille. Mr. Ponchaux owned a small general store next door, and the family lived on the second floor over the store. Neither of the two daughters, both teenagers, had ever seen an airman before, especially one from a foreign land.

"He had come to liberate us, but instead fell among us," Mr. Daubercies told the girls. Both girls were a little terrified at first, but it was not long before we were all chatting away in French. Josette was just about the prettiest young lady that I had ever seen, and I found myself very attracted to her. Soon there was some measure of mutual curiosity, from the smiles I began to receive. Along with the Daubercies, Josette certainly was to make life worth living while I was in Chauny.

On the second day of my stay, Mr. Daubercies showed me to my hiding place, to be used during any searches by unfriendly visitors. There was a small shed, behind the Ponchaux home, with straw strewn over the floor. Reaching into the straw, he pulled up a trap door exposing a flight of stairs. Climbing down, I found a small, dark, room which had been carved out of the earth. This was where I would stay while the visitors searched the houses and the grounds.

I was forced to use the room only once during my stay, but this was for nothing so serious as a house search. We had been visited by a buxom German nurse, who claimed to only want some friendly conversation. However, in Mr. Daubercies' opinion, the German women could often be worse than the men. Other than this nurse, few Germans ventured down Rue General Leclerc. In fact, the town of Chauny was unusually quiet, with few known house searches from the day of my arrival until my departure.

After the introductions, Josette and I began to spend a considerable amount of time together, particularly in the home of the Daubercies. We played cards much of the time, and most of the rest trying to upgrade our skills in each other's language. By the end of my stay in Chauny, I was speaking quite passable French, and Josette was speaking in a somewhat-halting English. My few trips away from the house were always with her as my companion. Apparently we gave the appearance of an ideal pair of lovers, and who would dare to interfere with that by arresting us? And, who was I to argue the point, when I had a pretty lady by my side?

After the second week of my stay, it was suggested that I was in need of a haircut. In France, long hair quite often indicated someone in hiding. Josette volunteered to take me to the barber shop, and so we set off, arm in arm. Past the town hall and through the central park we walked. Several German soldiers were passed, some on parade and some

The shed with the straw floor. Neal's hideout was underneath.

casually walking around town. We exchanged smiles and small talk with them; by this time I was getting proficient enough in the French language to get away with it. Not one of the soldiers asked for my papers, or even showed much curiosity about a young chap who was not off with some work party. To them, we were simply a pair of young lovers.

Just past the far side of the park, we came to a large house. On entering, we found a number of men and several young girls, all hard at work. This was the headquarters of the Resistance in Chauny. One of the young girls, about 17 years of age, was to be my barber. Her name was Ginette Logeon and she was surprisingly good at cutting hair. I found out she was also one of the main radio operators for the local Resistance cell, taking her turn to call London for instructions.

What produced the greatest surprise, however, occurred when she asked me to look out of the front window. All I saw was another large house across the street, with several men lounging around the front door. "Le Gestapo," she said, hardly showing any emotion. The house across the road was their headquarters for the whole region. It certainly took a lot of heroism to operate a clandestine radio, and barbershop for airmen on the run, just across the street from the German secret police.

When Ginette was done, Josette and I left the house and did another short tour of Chauny. Then we returned home to the Daubercies. It was certainly becoming obvious that Chauny was not one of the higher-security towns, as would have been the case closer to the seacoast. Nobody seemed to care how many airmen were hiding in this town.

Neal's "barber," Ginette Logeon-Just, in Brittany in 1991.

Life went on for several more weeks, during which Josette and I sharpened our skills at both language and rummy. We really seemed to be growing quite fond of one another, and I certainly hoped that I would be able to sit out the war right where I was. But, that was not to be, since very unfortunately, the Resistance had other plans for us.

There was plenty of anticipation over the upcoming second front. From the raids we had done through March and April, I knew it could not be far away; we had been softening up the French transportation system for this.

The barbershop and Resistance headquarters in Chauny. Across the street waited the Gestapo.

Now the radio messages to the Resistance told them that the landings were only a few days away. Then on June 5, we were advised that the Allies would be landing in two days. We would have to be ready for departure on that particular day; the Resistance did not want us in the town after the landings had taken place. They would not be able to help us after this since they would be too busy blowing up railroad lines.

Anticipating a good sleep on the night of June 5, we retired at our normal times. We were roused, early on the morning of the 6th, by a loud pounding on the front door. "Les Allies sont arrive," the stranger told us excitedly as we opened the door, "Nous partirons dans un demi-heure par camion." I rapidly got dressed, gathered all of my few belongings, and waited by the front door. Soon a small covered truck showed up, and after good-byes to the Daubercies, I climbed inside. I didn't even have a chance to say my farewells to Josette or her family.

The truck already held a number of young chaps, all airmen who had been hiding out in the same town as I. One was a RAF flyer who had been hiding for several years, had made himself right at home, and could speak French like a native. He had already known the region from before the war. We drove for about an hour out into the countryside until we came to a large farm near the village of Ugny le Gay. We would be staying there until the turmoil of the landings had subsided and it was safe to move us to other hideouts.

The farmer and his wife greeted us warmly and then showed us to our living quarters, the hay stacks in his large barn. We would be bedded down in the straw at night, but allowed the run of the house during daylight hours. There were seven of us by then, airmen from Canada, England, the U.S.A., and even a single New Zealander. We ate our meals in the large kitchen of the house. For the week that we were there, no strangers even came near the place, although we heard there was a raid by the German SS shortly after our departure.

This proved to be a really unusual family. The farmer was overly affectionate and insisted on kissing every one of us, on each cheek, whenever we entered, or left, his

The farmhouse in Bethancourt-En-Vaux. The evaders' room was just to the left of the door.

presence. This was not that big a deal in France, but what was unusual was the huge, bushy, moustache he sported. He strained his soup through this moustache, and the particles of food remaining behind proved less than attractive. His wife was attractive and friendly, and did her utmost to make us feel at home. She, fortunately, did not sport a moustache.

The remaining two inhabitants of the farm were the daughters. They were both in their upper teens, and both quite pretty. But that was where the attraction stopped for any of us. Both of the daughters were about as muscular and strong as any of us had ever seen before. Lifting 8-inch logs seemed nothing to either girl, and the way they handled their machinery was awesome. None of the seven airmen, young and strong as we seemed, wanted to start any wrestling matches with either of these young ladies. Nor, I might add, any love affairs.

When June 13 arrived, the truck returned for us. The panic was about over, now that the Normandy landings were more secure. All of the German efforts were being concentrated in pushing the Allies back into the sea. It was now safe to move us. Bob Lindsay and I were driven to the small village of Bethancourt en Vaux, about 10 miles outside of Chauny. We were dropped off at a small farm that was just inside the village.

Notes:

The canal was "Le Canal de St. Quentin" which meandered through the northwest corner of L'Aisne province.

At my last report, Pierre Daubercies was a judge in the city of Marseilles. His father died before I was able to make my first return in 1969, and his mother shortly after. The Ponchaux father died before 1969 and the mother about 10 years ago.

Josette is today Mrs. Serge Baudinot, and lives in Bourg la Reine, a suburb of Paris. Her husband was also in the Resistance, but in the Auvergne region, close to Clermont-Ferrand. I still kick myself for not making a greater effort.

Mireille, sister of Josette, is Mme. Mireille Henri of Paris. Divorced for many years, Mireille was the antithesis of her sister.

The Resistance line, known as the "Reseau Shelburne," would normally conduct us to the Cherbourg, or Breton, regions, where we would be taken off by submarine or boat. Once the Normandy landings occurred, it was decided to keep us in place until liberated.

Ginette Logeon was later to become Mrs. Ginette Logeon-Just, and a school teacher. She now lives in St. Vaast de Longmont, and enjoys her many grandchildren.

The Resistance had actually been told that the landings were coming on June 7. I think they were more surprised than the Germans.

From the embraces of the farmer, at Ugny le Gay, one of my pet tricks is to point a broom at someone, and say, "Want to kiss a Frenchman?" The seven airmen at the farm started this saying.

Chapter 11

The Farm

Our newest hideout was owned by a middle aged Belgian couple; Mr. and Mrs. Valeyre Reyns. They had owned the farm for many years and had apparently enjoyed a fair measure of prosperity. There were no children, but the Reyns were a jolly couple and really enjoyed our company while we were with them. And the feeling was mutual! Neither was much over 5 feet in height and, in the case of Mrs. Reyns, about the same in breadth. And the breadth was not all fat, as we were soon to learn to our chagrin.

On our first day we met the third member of our hiding team; Capt. John Kupsick, fondly known as Jack. A navigator from a B-17 Flying Fortress, of the U.S. 8th Air Force, he had been shot down the previous February. Wounded in the attack, Jack had spent several months in a French hospital being treated, and now was in the Resistance line awaiting liberation. However, we heard that he still carried a lot of lead in his body.

The first thing that the Reyns did after we arrived was to set down some of the ground rules. We could go outside of the house only after dark, and only then if there was nobody else around. We were expected to help with some of the housework, where possible, and a little of the farm work. If anybody came to visit, we were expected to stay in our room and remain quiet. We agreed to all the rules, as if we wanted to have any choice in the matter.

Our room was right off the parlor and dining room, and would house the three of us. It was a bit on the small side but held a double and a single bed. Bob and I, as crewmates, shared the double while Jack got the single. It had been great to have a room all to myself in Chauny, but this sharing was a new experience for me. The room was about half the size the one in Chauny, but with three times the residents. It did not take long for the confinement to start rattling our composures.

The three roommates in front of the farm, 1994. Shown from left are Neal, Bob Lindsay and Jack Kupsick.

Within a week, three otherwise rational guys were busy chasing and catching flies. If one of us caught five, he became an Ace. Then we started collecting corks, hollowing them out, and using straight pins, made our versions of POW camps for the flies. It was fortunate that our village did not have any of the guys with the white jackets.

Of course, much of the reason for our fly chasing was the sheer number of them. We had flies by the thousands in our little world. In order to get any sort of relief from them at night, we had to start what we called a "flap parade." We each took a towel and, starting in the corners, flapped our way to the door. As the last fly was chased out, we slammed the door and went to bed. This usually meant a fly-free night's sleep.

Except for one infamous night! Believing that all of the little creatures had gone, I fell into a deep sleep. Somewhere in the middle of the wee small hours, I awoke to something landing on my nose. I took a swipe at it, but the little nuisance kept coming back. After I had kept swinging at it for nearly an hour, I had had enough, and turned on the light. Opening my eyes, there was Lindsay, string in hand, and laughing his head off. I did not hand him over to the Germans that night, but it was pretty close.

Mrs. Reyns was a strong little person and reminded us of a somewhat more senior version of the girls from our last farm. One of our evening activities consisted of Indian arm wrestling, and it proved just about all any of us could do to out-wrestle the lady. Usually it was a stand-off. Still, these contests would normally be followed by a few rounds of our host's principal homemade liqueur. But more on this tipple, and tippling, later. First we have to talk about food.

Our breakfast, on most mornings, consisted of the standard French fare: cafe au lait, a few slices of baguettes, some butter and jam. The French did not subscribe to eggs or cereal for the morning meal, but the eggs were for later in the day. The coffee was homemade and we airmen soon learned to make it; true coffee was almost impossible to find in Europe at this time. Any suitable ingredient was applied to the making of ersatz coffee: dried beans, peas, barley or other coarse grains. These were put into a round canister and rotated over a hot fire until the roasting was completed. This usually took the better part of the day, so we did not lack for activities. With a little chicory added, and perhaps a tot or two of the scarce brandy, the product became an almost passable coffee.

With breakfast barely finished, we helped to start the preparations for lunch. One of the major tasks we had to perform was the peeling of the potatoes. Every day we peeled enough for both lunch and dinner for the five of us; a large bucket full. Now, with our collective years of service behind us, this should have been no major chore! But, the service did not grow their own potatoes, in the same way as did our host. The service did not dump the outhouse onto the potato garden, for fertilizer, as did our host. And the potatoes the service grew did not stink up our hands for days, the way our host's did. But this was a small price to pay for the fine taste of those potatoes.

Besides the potatoes, our lunch consisted of one of three types of meat, veal, rabbit or chicken, usually served in rotation. But helping at the preparation of the meat created whole new experiences for us. Shortly after our arrival, Mr. Reyns decided to slaughter and dress one of his calves. He asked us to lend a hand at the killing and slaughter, but of course he was required to do most of the work. Bob was the only farmer in the trio of airmen, and he had never killed calves. The carcass was cut up and stored in coarse salt to preserve the flesh.

For the first few weeks, the salt did just that; the veal was sweet and tender. After about a month, the colour began to change to a deeper red, and the flavor started downhill. Towards the end of July, the meat was almost inedible, but it was still put in front of us at lunch. We picked away at it, but with declining enthusiasm. Finally Mrs. Reyns considered it beyond hope, and out it went. Little regret was shown by any of us.

With the rabbit being a one-meal animal, we did not encounter the same problem here; it was always fresh meat. However, we were definitely expected to share in the killing, and this, rather than the flavor, gave us our major problem. I had tasted rabbit only once before, and with mixed feelings. However, at the Reyns, rabbit was an extremely tasty meal when served in a ragout. Unfortunately, we had to block out of our minds what we had done just hours earlier.

Shortly after breakfast, Mrs. Reyns picked out the rabbit for that day's lunch. Then the skin was cut around the neck and, with two of us pulling in opposite directions, we skinned the animal. It was, at this time, still alive and screaming! The rabbit went into the pot and the skin was sold to a fur dealer from town. I still feel guilty today when trying to look a rabbit in the eye.

The chicken was a much simpler task; I had seen my grandfather killing them many times, and this was not any different. However, to see our hostess, at lunch, picking away at chicken parts that we would have declared inedible, was unnerving. Even the head was not spared. Our evening meal almost always consisted of the leftover potatoes, fried in fat, and with about a dozen eggs broken over them. As good as everything else was, this usually tasted the best; and, probably added the most to my expanding waistline.

The farmer, besides raising calves, rabbits and chickens, had a herd of milk cows, and orchards of cherry and apple trees. During our stay, we were entering the picking season for both of these fruits, and again we were called on to assist. The cherry crop obtained most of our attention since the apples were not yet ripe. However, both of these played a key role in the farmer's major product line.

In his front yard was a large, very old, cider press that had seen many years of service. From this he produced plenty of cider, and with further processing, Calvados. This was a highly distilled form of apple liqueur, mainly native to Normandy. The taste of this was great but it was the Calvados that brought the cherries into play. The fresh-picked cherries were packed in large glass bottles, topped off with the Calvados, sealed, and put away for two years. This storage period created a cherry liqueur that was excellent, and probably caused a good many hangovers.

By late July, the cherry crop was ready for harvest. Mr. Reyns brought in two friends from Belgium to help out in the orchard. It would take about two weeks to complete the job. We were asked to pit the cherries as they came into the house. Sadly the farmer had not taken our tastes for the product into account, and I am certain he lost a larger percentage of his crop than normal. But we pitted enough to fill the bottles, and he topped them off with the Calvados. There would be a great party here in 1946!

The harvest helpers were from Ghent, and active in the Resistance forces of that area. We became quite good friends since they lived in the Reyns house during the harvest. They had a large supply of Belgian tobacco with them, which they offered to share with us. I don't know how it is different from other tobacco, but the instant I tried it, I thought I was going to lose the top of my head. In the pipe I then had, it was vile; in cigarettes only slightly better. The donor of the tobacco owned a hotel in Ghent, and he had a daughter that he was apparently trying to marry off.

He offered me a half-interest in the hotel if I would consider being part of the union. Then he showed me a picture of the daughter! Right away the tobacco started to taste a little better.

With the harvest over, they left for home, and life at the Reyns returned to normal. At least as normal as it could ever get in our little hiding place. Much of our idle days were spent looking out over the front courtyard and observing the day's activities that took place there. Many of the villagers came for milk, which our host sold, and this activity gave us some idea of the neighbors. We did speculate about a few of them. One lady, obviously in a family way, was a regular, but very close to giving birth. Whenever she arrived, she had grown just a little bit larger. Surely she could not have many more weeks to go. As a pastime, the three of us made up a lottery on the date of delivery. Surprisingly, and probably very timely, she had a baby boy on the same day as our liberation. Jack won the pot, but never stayed around to collect.

There were a couple of young girls who came around most days for milk, but they never did receive a good reception from our host. They had been seen regularly in the company of German soldiers, and this was certainly frowned on in this town. Several wars had already been fought, against Germany over this piece of land that they lived on. There was not very much love lost here for the Germans, or for anyone who collaborated with them.

Then there were the dogs; a male that came to visit the bitch that lived on the farm. Ours was quite old, but the male still found her attractive. So this one day, away they went, right in the middle of the front yard. After a few minutes of passion, the dogs were inseparable. They just stood there, looks of complete innocence on their faces, while we laughed. Then a bucket of cold water solved the passion problem.

Jack was a little older than either Bob or I, and had seen quite a bit more of life, or so he said. His home was in Great Falls, Montana, and he told us of the days spent running liquor over the border from Alberta. (Today, he denies it!) We were seeing quite a lot of his U.S. Air Force buddies now. The B-17 bombers, high overhead, were heading deep into Germany on their bombing missions. We also saw plenty of Mustang (P-51) and Lightning (P-38) fighters cruising around, often unmolested by the German fighters. There were occasional dogfights with ME-109's or FW-190's of the Luftwaffe, and the results of these did not always end up in a win by the U.S. fighters, at least not on one occasion.

One day, an American Mustang was chased across Bethancourt en Vaux by a FW-190, and just about half a mile from us, the starboard wing of the Mustang parted from the fuselage. The pilot managed to bail out, at little more than 1,000 feet altitude, and the plane crashed around the edge of the village. The pilot fell directly into Resistance hands and was quickly hidden in one of the houses of the village. When we met him a few days later, he, as a captain, was quite busy trying to take over as Commandant of Evaders. We soon let him know that he was far too wet behind the ears for any command jobs. With his plane so close to town, the villagers flocked to the site searching for souvenirs. By the time the Germans arrived, there was little left for them to salvage.

There was one rumor going around about a P-38 fighter, from a group flying nearby, who had engine problems. The pilot landed the plane in a nearby field, fixed up his problems, and took off again. The other planes circled the area to give the first pilot protection. This would take a lot of daring, even though the German Luftwaffe was no longer a major threat.

But the Germans on the ground were still active and, on one occasion, caused us to retreat into hiding. Mr. Reyns had a large haystack made up with bales. One of the bales was loose, and by lifting it just right, we could climb into the small space underneath. There was only just room enough for the three of us, with a little airspace. Word of the impending search came through one day and we quickly climbed into our hiding space. The soldiers searched the farm, even probing into the bales with their bayonets. Fortunately for us, but especially the Reyns, they found nothing. Shortly after, the soldiers went on to search another house, and we returned to ours.

Our body cleansing habits at the farm were, to say the least, rather primitive. There was little of toilet facilities in the house, and the outhouse was only visited when we were unobserved. It received the most attention from us only after dark. Getting ourselves into a state that would pass for clean was something of a major chore. Without a bathroom, our daily wash and shave was confined to a bucket on the kitchen table. Only once a week could we go for a major cleanup, and this was while our hosts were away at church on Sunday morning.

Once they had left, we started to fill up a large tub with hot water, and then we had our baths in rotation, and in the same water. While one was bathing, the others were either shaving or brushing their teeth. The biggest contest was to see who got the hot water first, while it was still clean. Occasionally I was lucky enough to win the clean water, but then, of course, I had to shave and brush my teeth in used water. All this was supposed to keep us clean for the week.

On one such Sunday morning, we were treated to a little more than we had expected from our cleanings. On this morning, we became so wrapped up in the procedures that we failed to take the usual precautions; we forgot to close the blinds. Suddenly, one of us looked up and spotted the two young girls watching us from the pathway. They were standing 50 or so feet from us, and laughing their heads off at a bunch of guys, totally in the nude and just beginning to turn beet red. On any other day, and in any other location, they would have been invited inside. But not today! We simply closed the blinds and hoped we had not been seen by anybody who would inform on us.

While there were few collaborators in the village, there were a lot more in the town of Chauny. Among these was a jeweller who had rented rooms from the Reyns at about the time the Americans started bombing Chauny. He felt his family would be safer in the country than in the town. At first they used the rooms only on weekends but, after the middle of August, with the Allied armies approaching ever closer, they stayed all week. The jeweller had befriended the Germans, and done regular business with them. His wife was of the same stripe. They had one young son with them.

While the collaborators were using the rooms, we evaders had to stay very quiet, so as not to give ourselves away. We could only leave the room for meals or after dark. By late August, we were staying in the room all the time, except for meals. Had they known we were there, the collaborators would have turned us all in to the Germans. For us as Allied airmen, it would have meant the POW camps; for the Reyns, it would have meant the firing squad.

The back of the farmhouse. The room at the left was where the evaders were when several girls happened to catch them bathing.

Notes:

The coffee (?) became even better with a tot of Calvados added to it.

Mr. Reyns, and the rest of us, didn't realize it then, but he was a leader in the science of natural fertilizers. Unfortunately, outhouses have become virtually extinct.

There was a huge market for rabbit fur in France. Fortunately, Brigit Bardot had not yet taken on an activist role.

I still like eggs on my fried potatoes, so I had better learn to like my expanded waistline.

One of the better tours today is through Normandy, tasting some of the great Calvados along the way. I have, since the war, had bottles of homemade product from the Chauny region. Some of this is 80 percent ethanol, so it can be used to replace gasoline in an emergency.

Based on my much misspent life since the war, I should have given a little more thought to the offer. After all, the hotel was rather attractive.

Jack proved a rather elusive person after we parted company. It took me until 1991, in Irvine, CA, before I found him again. Seems he was too busy fighting other wars for me to find him. But we made up for the wait, and after a session in Toronto in September 1995, He is now my brother-in-law.

We watched the dogfight from the back kitchen window. None of us thought about the bullets that missed the Mustang, and could have hit us.

I should have gone after the collaborators for interfering with the flow of natural fertilizer.

The Maquis-The French Resistance-in hiding, but not too worried to forget haircuts.

Chapter 12

THE ROAD TO LIBERATION

By the time the collaborators had moved onto the farm full time, the Allied armies were only just over the horizon. Paris had already been liberated and the German army pushed far beyond in its rush to escape to the Rhine. We were right in their path. We could hear the guns firing and air activity was increasing almost daily. It would be only a few days until the Germans would be gone, and the region we were in liberated. Evacuations of non-essential personnel already were underway. Finally the end of August arrived, and with it our liberators.

We had been watching the flashes of the guns at night, and heard many of the shells passing overhead; we could hardly wait to see the first of the "Friendly Faces." On the night of Aug. 31, we went to bed at our usual time, trying hard to sleep despite the constant shelling going on around us. Around 2 a.m., we were roused by Mr. Reyns, who beckoned for us to follow him outside. We filed out of the house, across the yard, and into the large barn overlooking the back road. Looking through one of the windows, and onto the road, an incredible sight greeted us.

Hundreds, or more likely, thousands, of German soldiers were fleeing to the east along the road. Some were walking, many were running and a few pedaled along on bicycles. There was not a sign of any kind of motorized transport for any of these fleeing soldiers. What also was quite significant was that very few of them carried any arms. We were, quite evidently, witnessing a rout. But, without trucks, not too many of them would get very far. Somewhere about 4 a.m., the last of them passed our vantage point. From then on, an eerie silence descended on the village and we sensed we were totally alone. Even the guns were suddenly silenced. So, back to bed we went, anticipating the Allied armies in the coming morning.

Dawn had scarcely broken when we were again roused from sleep. The guns had started up again and we could hear shells whistling over the house. Valeyre ran into our room shouting that the Allies had arrived. Again we went with him, at his beckoning. This time we were handed shovels, and at a plot, some 50 feet from the house, we were told to dig. A foot or so down, we uncovered a cache of liquor that Valeyre had hidden four years ago, as the Germans were approaching. The bottles had waited all this time for just such an occasion as this. We brought them into the house, set them down on the kitchen table, and settled down to fulfill the obligation!

At about 10 a.m., we heard the first clanking of vehicles out back of the barn. Rushing out, we found part of the U.S. Army, the 347th Engineering Corps, moving slowly along the road. By now we had had our fill of the buried liquor, and were really unable to offer much of a dignified welcoming committee for the liberating soldiers. Still we did the best we could; climbing all over the personnel carriers and singing a very off-key version of "O Canada." From the looks on their faces, perhaps the Americans felt they were listening to our version of "Deutschland Uber Alles." Because they didn't unsling their weapons, we'll never be really certain what they thought. But they were certainly a very welcome sight to us, and the citizens of the village. We asked them if they would join our party, now going on, but the lieutenant of the unit said that they still had other villages to liberate.

So, back we went into our house, and allowed them to proceed on their way. After all, a good party, once started, had to be maintained at all costs, especially during an occasion such as this.

We were finally free! No more hiding out in haystacks or dugout rooms! No more keeping quiet because of the collaborators! The townsfolk all flocked to the farm to meet us; all but the pregnant lady. She was, at this very moment, delivering her new baby. The jeweler's wife, and the two collaborating girls, were brought out onto the street. While the girls cried, and the wife loudly proclaimed her loyalty to France, they had their hair chopped off. Now baldheaded, the three took off, and the party really started. The jeweler himself was turned over to the authorities, and goodness know what fate awaited him.

We visited many of the neighborhood homes and shared in their toasting of the liberation, and the liberating armies. Much later, Valeyre brought out a prewar auto, and we took off towards Chauny. Part of the way there, we got into another party; this one engrossed us for what was left of the day, and a good part of the night. Rather than stagger on into Chauny, we retraced our steps to Bethancourt and stayed the balance of the night with the Reyns.

The following day, after a tearful farewell with the Reyns, the three evaders left for Chauny. The town was having a whopper of a party when we arrived, having only been liberated the day before. Mrs. Daubercies welcomed me into her home, and I was moved into the same bedroom as before. Josette had brought out her Junior Red Cross uniform, and she looked even prettier than before. There was a big liberation parade planned for the next day, and we evaders were to be given a place of honour in it. So the parties carried on until the morning of the parade. Everybody had brought out the booze that had been hoarded for so many years. From the way we were going at it, it would not last a whole lot longer!

Sept. 3 dawned wet and cloudy. But nobody cared about the state of the weather; we were having a parade! After breakfast with the Daubercies, and a few glasses of cognac to sustain us through all the excitement, we set off for the assembly point. There were about 33 evaders from the area taking part in this parade; we were from many different countries. One was even a Russian soldier who had escaped shortly after the invasion of his country. He made it quite obvious that he was in no hurry to go home; he liked what he had seen in this one.

The parade started out, with the evaders right up near the head of the column. Behind us were the members of the Resistance, then the French Army, and then anyone else that

The liberation parade in Chauny, Sept. 3, 1944. Bob Lindsay is on the extreme right; Neal is fourth from the right, wearing a beret. Resistance member Entienne Dromas is behind them, wearing a neck scarf.

wanted to take part. The whole parade wound on for about a mile. As we passed each bistro or restaurant, the proprietors would run out and hand us bottles of liquor or wine. Being at the front meant we managed to receive the best of it all. And there were a lot of bistros and restaurants along the route of the parade. Just as we were about to pass the last one in town, somebody announced that we were on our way to church..

This was to be the highlight of the parade; a blessing from the local Bishop. But would he really go ahead and bless 33 drunken evaders? Sure enough, right into the church we marched, and took over the first two rows of pews. Hardly one of us could see who was giving the blessing, but we were getting it just the same. Had my mother been here to see me, on this day, I would have been disowned by the family. Still, there were others in the church that day in conditions similar to ours. I would presume that the local priests must have spent many hours, later that week, listening to confessions.

After the sermon, Josette gathered me in and helped me home to the Daubercies. They had a great banquet planned for that evening. I managed to sober up enough to enjoy that feast, and later to discuss our futures. I was starting back for England the following day, and the others were taking up their lives again, hopefully where they left off in 1940. Josette and I talked about any possibility of a life together, but she was reluctant to come to Canada. If I was able to get back to Chauny, we could then see what would happen. I did not know what the Air Force had in store for me.

I suppose that Josette's initial reluctance to emigrate to my country was probably the major reason behind my failure to return to France until 1969. By then, it was far too late for us.

The evaders at the English Cemetery, Chauny, after the parade. Bob Lindsay is in the center of the front row; Neal is third from the right in the back row.

Notes:

I can sympathize with the husband and his collaboration. The worst of the occupying forces would be hard-pressed to outdo his wife. She was a harridan as a collaborator, and a harridan when she later became a French patriot. Actually, she was much prettier with her hair shaved off. But, that God-awful voice!

Collaborators were people who played "footsy" with the Germans, while retaining the stance of being the true patriots of France. Mostly they were the low end of the achiever scale.

All female collaborators received a head shave after the liberation. It was a common sight to see bald women for some time after France was free. The men normally received jail sentences or, in exceptional circumstances, the supreme penalty.

I returned to Bethancourt en Vaux in 1969, to see the Reyns. However, they had sold the farm and returned to Belgium. Both died some years later.

Josette was a member of the French Junior Red Cross, and what she did for that uniform should never have been allowed. But then, I was only a red-blooded girl watcher!

Chapter 13

THE ROAD HOME

The following morning, after another very tearful farewell, I started out on foot towards what I hoped would finally be Paris. Along the way, I joined up with an American air gunner who was also going to the same place. We walked along together until we passed through the outskirts of Chauny, and on to the highway going southwest towards Paris. It was a long way, and we hoped to pick up a ride to get us there.

A few miles beyond the edge of Chauny, a U.S. Military Police jeep pulled up alongside us. After asking for our identity, and our dog tags, which we had surrendered to the Resistance, the soldiers asked us to get into the jeep. From there they took us to a nearby farm which was the local MP headquarters. They asked us more questions, but there was no way we could prove our stories. A few German infiltrators were still in the system and they had to be certain that none escaped the net. So we would stay with them until they were certain of our identities.

There I was, free from the threat of being a POW in Germany, only to be made a POW by our Allies, the Americans. They escorted us forward, almost to the front lines, where we were added to a group of 75 German prisoners who had just been collected. For a couple of days we drove around the lines with these prisoners before starting out again for Paris. We were at times within range of the German guns. What a fate I was staring at; evading the Germans successfully for five months, made a prisoner by the Americans, and killed by the Germans after liberation! Very fortunately, they were never quite able to find the range.

To get the two of us back into uniform, we were invited to help ourselves to clothing from a pile near the camp. Picking through the heap, I was not able to find anything in Air Force blue, and did not fancy myself as a footslogging GI. But beggars could not be choosers at this point, and I was soon decked out as a master sergeant in the U.S. Army. A little later we were told that these clothes had come from soldiers who had been killed or wounded in action.

The 75 German prisoners captured during recent actions were the saddest looking group of men I had ever seen. They were mainly young boys or old men. One of them who could speak a little English said he had only been on a holiday from his home in Switzerland, when he was conscripted. There were no overt Nazis in this group. After a couple of days together, we were all piled onto trucks and added to a convoy heading west. Our destination was a processing camp just west of Paris. Our only night stopover was just outside the town of Laon, our target on the night I was shot down. It was something of a thrill to see the place where I had become a Caterpillar five months earlier.

The next day we carried on towards Paris. By now there was little doubt in the minds of the guards that we were legitimate evaders, and we were separated from the other prisoners. They put the two of us in a small pup trailer which was being towed by a larger truck. We were not quite by ourselves; there was a substantial supply of American cigarettes traveling with us. We did not question why the cigarettes were coming away from the front, where they were really needed, but made certain some of them were well-used back here.

The convoy arrived in Paris about suppertime, and drove leisurely through the downtown area on its way west. When it stopped for a moment at an intersection, we two evaders jumped off the trailer without giving it a second thought. Well, we did think to liberate a few of the cigarettes, and each took three cartons with him. Dashing across the road, we barged into a handy bistro, and sat down at the bar. Before we were able to catch our breath, or hide from anyone chasing us, we found a round of drinks in front of us. The other patrons of the bar were showing an interest in us, and we were soon in a conversation with one and all. I had finally made it to Paris, after all these months!

We told our stories to the bar patrons and, before we knew it, we were surrounded by a whole crowd of friendly people. After our tales were finished, we were treated like visiting royalty. One of the first patrons we had met then invited us to go with him to his mother's apartment. She was having a celebration party that same evening, and we were now invited to go. At this party, we enjoyed plenty of champagne and excellent food, among these newly found friends. I had to admit that the French were very adaptable; Paris had only been liberated two weeks earlier. While not too much else was working in this city, the hospitality was certainly very much in place!

Much later in the evening, we said our goodbyes to our hostess, and started the search for a place to sleep. Not too far away we found a hotel, or at least one that appeared to be just that. They would rent us rooms providing we did not interfere with their normal clientele. But the knocks on the door as we tried to fall asleep told us where we were: a brothel. Some choice for our first night in Paris! It was all a very tempting idea, but not so much of an idea as a good night's sleep, after the haystacks we had slept in for the past few days.

The following morning, the American and I parted company. He was going to his headquarters and I was going across town to the home of Pierre Daubercies. His mother gave me the address, and suggested I stay there while I was in Paris. The walk gave me my first view of the Eiffel Tower as I passed close by it. Arriving at Pierre's apartment, 10 or 15 blocks further on, I rang the bell, and met Pierre.

Pierre was actually a tenant in the apartment of a postman and his wife. It was not a very big apartment but they would make room for me while I stayed. Pierre was attending classes all day, but the postman worked only mornings, with the rest of the day off. That night we all went to the Moulin Rouge restaurant to celebrate our new-found friendship. This was the first restaurant I had ever visited during my stay in France, and it was significant that it was among their very best.

The postman spent his afternoons acting as my tour guide to Paris. Together we saw almost everything worth seeing; the Louvre, Notre Dame cathedral, Sacre Coeur cathedral, Place de la Concorde, Arc de Triumphe, le Champs Elysees, etc. All of this was done strictly on foot since the Metro was not yet operating. In peacetime, this week's tour would have set me back many dollars. I really should have reported in to the Air Force headquarters by this time, but who knew if I would ever be able to do this again? So I wanted to visit everything I could possibly see, while I was in the "City of Lights."

Mr. and Mrs. Daubercies are on the right, with Pierre Daubercies in the center. Others in the photo are friends of the family. Pierre Daubercies is now a French judge.

At the end of a week, I moved out of the apartment and reported to RCAF headquarters. These were located in the Hotel George V, right across the street from the Place de L'Opera. It was said to be just about the finest hotel in Paris at the time, and the quarters to which I was assigned certainly did not disprove this. Located on the same floor as the reception area, the bedroom was massive! It contained a huge bed, for my sole use. The bathroom itself was bigger than the bedroom at the Reyns. It was sheer luxury living! Even better still, I soon found out I would be here for at least another week, since there was no air transport to London available at the moment. The airplanes could stay away for a year, as far as I was concerned.

On the second day of my stay, I went through a complete interrogation from one of the Air Intelligence officers. He wanted to know what I had done since being shot down, and the people who had helped me. He advised that these people were to be compensated for their help to downed airmen. During the interrogation, I found out about the balance of the crew. Bob Lindsay had already gone through and was back in England. Vic Knox, the tail gunner, was the only fatal casualty, and was probably killed during the attack. Pat Murphy and J.D. Thompson were captured, and made POWs. Arnold Greene, and Chuck Thomas though seriously wounded, had made it through France to Spain, Gibraltar, and on to Britain. Arnold had given a report about an enemy fighter being shot down, and a fight with German SS troops on the ground. I did not have the chance to observe any of these events, and was happy not to have participated.

After this, I was given an allowance of 2,000 French francs and this, with the 1,000 francs of escape money I still had, should create a bit of fun in Paris. Unfortunately, I went on a gift-buying trip the following day; something for the family at home. When this was over, there was very little left over for any kind of fun. Even in these days, Paris was an expensive place to shop.

I was, however, fortunate enough to meet up with an American Army sergeant on leave, one who was loaded with money. Looking for someone to share his leave, he offered to treat anywhere we went throughout the city. When asked what I would most like to do, I replied with a rather embarrassed grin that I had not slept with a woman since Britain. This was the exact kind of adventure that he had on his mind.

We were directed to one of the finest brothels in Paris, where we relaxed away the rest of the day. The sergeant paid for the works! The place had obviously catered to the very highest German officers before the Allies came along. Quite a comedown for the ladies, to have a couple of sergeants to comfort, after becoming used to generals.

On another evening, another Canadian airman and I met a pair of young ladies in a bistro. After a couple of drinks, and a few dances, we set off to take them home. When we stopped at a park bench to neck a little, there was a sudden clamor not far away from us. Shots and voices were heard, so the four of us took off in different directions. We never did get together again. There were still a number of German troops hiding in the Paris sewer system, and they came up occasionally to create havoc. It had certainly worked with us!

Finally the end of the wonderful week arrived. A large contingent of ex-evaders were taken out to Le Bourget airport, and loaded onto a DC-3 Dakota airplane. The airport was still very much in ruins from the pounding it had taken during the city's liberation. However, the plane took off and within an hour we were approaching London. After landing, we were trucked into the city and reported to the Air Force headquarters. Here we received our back pay and a clothing allowance to buy new uniforms. Later that day, I sent a cable home to tell Mom and Dad that I was safe in London.

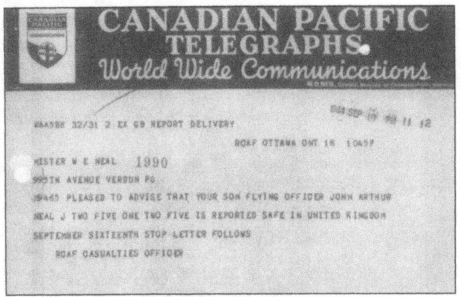

The telegram to Neal's family announcing his arrival in England.

By the following day, after a visit to Bond Street, I was again a flying officer, and no longer a master sergeant in the U.S. Army. A little later I was given two weeks' leave and told to report to Warrington for embarkation home. I asked several times to be allowed to finish my tour of operations, but was refused. I had been too long a member of the Resistance, and knew too many names. That France had been almost totally liberated by then didn't matter; I was being sent home.

I also asked about Edna, to whom I had proposed just before being shot down, but nobody at RAF headquarters could locate her whereabouts without her service number. I had forgotten to ask her for this detail when we were together. So, after a few days in London, I took the train back to Middleton St. George to see if anyone I knew was still there. The only one still active was P/O Edwards, and he was just finishing up his tour. My belongings had been sent on to a collection point, but a gold cigarette case, given to me by my parents, was possessed by my batwoman. She returned it to me. So, with the leave winding up, I took off for Warrington and home.

I had survived my greatest adventure, and now looked forward to new ones to come. There were many of these, but none ever matched my tour of occupied France. Unfortunately, because of circumstances, and perhaps my own stupidity, I lost out on the two most attractive ladies that I had ever known.

Notes:

I managed to recross tha Atlantic again early in 1945, to join another crew, but never recrossed the Channel. I blew my second and last chance, since Josette married Sgt. Serge Baudinot of the French Army in 1946. Serge retired from the Army as a captain and highly-decorated soldier in 1975. They have two sons, Jean-Marc and Laurent, and five grandchildren.

The people who helped out the evaders were supposed to receive compensation by the victorious governments. However, like many of our government promises, they reneged, and few of these people received a penny for their efforts. But, in most cases, the helpers felt that they owed us, and not the reverse.

I can't remember her name, but she claimed to be married, and working in a brothel to support the family. And who was I to argue, since there were few other ways of earning a living in Paris at the time. Anyway, she was blonde, and very attractive, and the room was decorated in an Arabian Nights theme, and I had been celibate long enough.

The locomotive on our way home from "Blighty" in June 1945.

On our way home in June 1945 and our welcoming committee.

Chapter 14

THE VETERAN

My great adventure was finally over! Feeling really let down, I spent almost a month around England, looking up old friends, old stations, and trying to relive old memories. Finally I checked into Warrington, getting ready to go back to Canada. My share of WWII was over.

Theoretically, I'm going home for leave. Although I requested it several times, they would not let me finish the tour I was on. Five months later, they apparently forgot about this rule.

Warrington was a holding station for airmen on their way home. We had no training activities to perform, and all of our time was our own. Most of this was used in the mess, trying our luck at gambling. And mine was all bad; I collected 10 pounds at pay parade one day, and half an hour later it was gone on the crap table. I may have been very lucky in the air, but please don't ask me to try the gambling tables.

After 10 days of holding, a ship was available at Greenock near Glasgow, and we all piled into the train heading that way. Waiting on the Firth of Clyde, ready to take me home, was the huge ocean liner, the *Queen Mary*. Never before had I seen any ship this big. Sailing out on a tender, we boarded our new home. This time it was no salon, but a stateroom shared with 8 or 10 other airmen going home.

The *Queen Mary* was like a big city; it just never seemed to end. It was crowded with homecoming troops and airmen, and quite a smattering of service-women. The food was just excellent, and with the fine weather at first, it felt more like a cruise that we were on. About five or six days after sailing, we pulled into Newark port, and then traveled north by train to Rockliffe Air Base at Ottawa.

I was posted here while they decided what to do with me next. First I received a month's disembarkation leave, and went home to Verdun. I arrived home to a rather unusual sight: my mother had a case of beer waiting for me. It was rather an emotional welcome from the family, since they

Josette and Serge Baudinot, Monique and Pierre Bauset (an evader), on the port bridge of the Queen Mary, 1991. It was here that Neal served watch on his return to Canada in 1944.

had not known my fate for over five months. But Mom was so happy that her son was alive, she threw over one of her usual vows. She had been to a church meeting that morning, where they had discussed prohibition, and on the way home, stopped into the local beer store, and bought me a dozen. This was the first time she had ever been in the store. Her friend, Mrs. Thompson, did the same for her son, Clayton, who had been on the ship with me.

Although total abstainers, both ladies were realists, knowing that we had been overseas and exposed to the "evils" of drink. But later that day, Mom discovered me enjoying the beer on our front balcony. She let me know, in no uncertain terms, that her sudden liberalization did not extend to the full view of all the neighbors.

After the leave was over, I spent some time on staff, but mostly just visiting night clubs in Ottawa and Hull — and often getting into trouble, as a result of the high proportion of ladies in the capital city region. Probably the best thing that the Air Force did for me was to move me on to my next posting.

Later I was assigned to a staff position at Lachine Manning Depot, where I had done my first training for the Air Force. Outside of the minimum requirements for this job, most of my time was spent touring the night clubs of the Montreal area. It was really a period, during which less was accomplished than during any other phase of my life, before or after. However, I did get to know the clubs quite well.

It was getting to the point where drink was presenting a problem. The adventure just finished was still fresh in my mind, and this sedentary life was no match for that. Drink was an every night affair, as it was with most of the airmen stationed at Lachine. I even had to help the station Padre to his bed one evening, after I had found him passed out in a field.

This was when I decided to take another stab at the career I had found so satisfying, but incomplete, up until now. Late in February 1945, I received a telegram advising of my impending discharge from the RCAF. While I was aware that the war in Europe was winding down, and aircrew needs at a minimum, I had the desire to extend my life in uniform as long as possible. Besides, I was now making more as a flying officer than I would as a machinist apprentice.

Having a friend in the Repat Depot who was allocating flyers for the few remaining needs in Britain, I requested that my name be put on a draft. In this case, friendship paid off, and very shortly I found myself on the way to Moncton Y Depot. I was going overseas again. A few days here and we went on to Halifax and boarded the *Mauretania*.

The identity card issued to Neal by the RAF on his return from France. Note that he still is wearing a master sergeant's uniform given to him by American troops, with his first lieutenant's bar on the right collar.

At Bournemouth, I crewed up with a Flying Officer Roberts and his crew. Then, after some days of getting acquainted, they sent us off to another heavy conversion unit at Wombleton, to get us into shape for a tour of operations.

We did a complete conversion unit course here, but half-way through, the war ended with the surrender of the German forces. We heard about this one day as we were finishing a cross-country trip. It was May 7, 1945. With the exercise over, we crossed the airfield just as all kinds of rockets came shooting up. A huge bonfire was burning in the centre of the field, and crowds of people were running everywhere.

Neal with sisters Joyce, Shirley and Dorothy on his return home in 1944.

The war was over! The CO had ordered the bonfire, and that every bottle and barrel of drinkable liquids be brought to midfield. And then the station celebrated the victory. Not too many survived the party without a hangover. We celebrated the victory, both on and off the base, and then finished the conversion course. After this, we were posted to 425 "Alouette" Squadron.

The Alouette was at Tholthorpe, Yorkshire. On our arrival, we were asked to volunteer for the Tiger Force, which was the members of Bomber Command who would go to the Pacific theatre to help fight Japan. The crew all volunteered. So we all came back to Canada, bringing our Lancasters with us, and settled into Debert to train for our new war.

However, we were barely settled into Debert when the Enola Gay dropped the big bomb on Hiroshima. This dictated the official end of my Air Force career, and now I just had to wait my turn for discharge. Because of the large number of airmen awaiting their return to civilian life, I had a few months yet to go. The pilot, navigator and wireless operator flew our Lancaster out to Alberta, and the rest of us waited around Debert for the final posting. Finally about October, I was moved on to Moncton for final processing.

This took about a month and a half because of all the others waiting, and the medical exams we had to go through, but finally on Nov. 30, 1945, I was free. I was once more a civilian. My nine months since my first notice of discharge at Lachine had produced nothing notable in my career. However, as I was to find later, these nine months were vital during my striving to achieve a higher education.

The highlight of my service career, and the event that paved my course in civilian life, came on the final day. With my discharge papers carefully tucked away, I climbed onto the train in Moncton, going home to Montreal. Sitting across from an attractive senior lady, we soon had a lively conversation going. She lived in Montreal and had been to Halifax to visit her sailor sons.

As we became better acquainted, we discussed my future now that I was out of the service. My plans had included a return to the locomotive shops to finish my apprenticeship. But she extolled the advantages of a university education, and I had plenty of reestablishment credits to cover this. I would get one free month of university for every month spent in the Air Force. With about 45 months in uniform, this would just about see me to my degree.

By the time of our arrival in Montreal, I was convinced. While the Allies may have won the war, this decision, made as the result of a conversation with a lovely lady, won my share of the peace.

So ended my great military service life! I would like to think that the Allied forces would have been repulsed without my participation, but this is foolish thinking. So I accepted it as an important phase of my life, and then went on to the next. By January 1946, I was launched into the search for higher education. And, a few years later, with the railroads converting from steam to diesel, my original career plans were rendered quite obsolete.

As one author wrote, during the production of my life story for his book, "John Neal was one lucky guy." I kind of agree!

Notes:

The senior lady, and I remained friends after reaching Montreal, but this did not last a very long time because of my dress code. Having never bought a civilian suit prior to joining up, my taste was suspect. When I showed up for a luncheon date looking like a member of Mafia, the lady was not impressed. It took a few more years before I attained any measure of style.

It took me about 49 years but I finally located Edna Tomlinson. She had served with the RAF until 1947, and a year after discharge, married Barney Leamon, an airman with whom she had been stationed. They now live in Norwich, England, and have two daughters and three grandchildren.

Josette and I are great friends, and I am invited to stay at their home in Bourg la Reine whenever I am in the Paris area. The same applies with Jean Hallade of Marizelle, whenever I am in the Chauny region.

Some of the survivors at a reunion of aircrew, September 1992. I am second from right, with my beer mug raised high.

Trying on the flying gear, 50 years later.

John Neal and Josette Baidinot at escaper's reunion.

Epilogue

The Final Count

In January 1992, the Canadian Broadcasting Corp. aired a trio of WWII documentaries under the title of "The Valor and the Horror." These documentaries were co-produced by the National Film Board of Canada, with the McKenna brothers, Brian and Terrence, as the main producer and commentator.

Two of the documentaries covered Canadians in the battles of Hong Kong and Normandy. While both had their critics among veterans, the most criticism was reserved for the third, titled "Death by Moonlight." This video described the bombing campaign over Europe by the RAF Bomber Command, and the part played in it by Canadians.

In it, we are described as either very callous and brutal flyers, or else very naive flyers. Led by A.V.M. Sir Arthur Harris, we were reputedly ordered to concentrate our bombs on the civilian population, at the expense of what were the more strategic military targets. As the crewmember responsible for the bombs, and their delivery to the target, I do not recall such an order.

Perhaps my story takes a somewhat "Polyanna-ish" look at the life of the author, during my four years as an airman. Perhaps, in the dark of the night, it is difficult to distinguish the valid from the invalid as targets. And perhaps our going out over Europe night after night with horrible losses did not equate to the damage or casualties we created.

But nowhere in this video is it mentioned the heavy damage caused by the German bombing of Great Britain. They did not tell of the staggering losses sustained by the British people, and the break up and scattering of families. Nothing was said of the indiscriminate sinking of ships and the killing of their crews, or the uncontrolled buzzbombs and V-1 rockets sent to terrorize the survivors. And this was only on the British Isles.

The horrors visited on the Russians, the Jews and on many of the German-occupied countries will never be fully recounted. Over 40 million people failed to survive the Nazi Holocaust, all because one little man wanted more "liebensraum."

No matter how many German civilians we killed, how many buildings we flattened, or how many factories we leveled, we need not suffer one twinge of conscience. The "Book of War" is too one-sided for that. So is the video! Where our concerns should lie is in never allowing such wars to happen again.

The writer's story is simply the account of his adventure when, as a young man, he was called on (more likely coerced) to serve his King and Country. If stories such as his are the scenarios of killers and murderers, then our world is really in trouble.

A photo of the six ex-evaders who were in the Chauny region of France, taken Sept. 1, 1994, during the celebrations of the 50th anniversary of liberation. Shown from left are RCAF navigator Bob Lindsay, Neal, USAF bombardier John Harms, the mayor of the town, USAF navigator John A. Kupsick, RAF pilot Stanley Knowles, USAF gunner Virgil Marco, and three unnamed former members of the French Resistance.

RCAF Friends and Casualties

"They Shall Grow Not Old"

Classmates from #1 B&G School, Jarvis, and #1 AOS, Malton, Ontario

Of the 18 students that finished the bombing and gunnery course, plus the air observer school where we received our wings, eight (44.5 percent) were killed in action, or on training, later during the war. These casualties were as follows:

Cutler, Eric Herrington P/O (BA) — KIA Feb. 20, 1944, age 20; #431 Iroquois Squadron, target - Leipzig. Buried in Berlin War Cemetery, Charlottenburg, Germany.

Mallette, Henri Clovis P/O (BA) — KIA May 23, 1944, age 25; #425 Alouette Squadron, target - LeMans. Buried in West Cemetery, LeMans Sarthe, France.

McCreary, James Duncan P/O (BA) — KIA March 31, 1944, age 25; #514 Squadron, target - Nuremberg. Buried in War Cemetery, Rheinberg, Germany.

Panton, Charles Lawrence P/O (BA) — KIA March 20, 1944, age 22; #192 Squadron, target - French Coast. Fate unknown, listed on the Runnymede War Memorial.

Preston, Stuart Marvin F/O (BA) — KIA May 13, 1944, age 21; #431 Iroquois Squadron, target - Louvain, Belgium. Buried in Brussels town cemetery, Evere-les-Bruxelles.

Smalley, Ronald Whitehead WO1 (BA) — KIA July 22, 1944; #582 Pathfinder Squadron, target - Kiel, Germany. Buried in Kril War Cemetery, Schleswig-Holstein, Germany.

Szymanski, Chester F/O (BA) — KIA June 22, 1944, age 22; #57 Squadron, target - Wesseling, Germany. Buried in War Cemetery, Rheinberg, Germany.

Trueman, Harry George F/O (BA) — KIA Jan. 31, 1944, age 24; #1660 Heavy Conversion Unit, training exercise. Buried in St. Germaine churchyard, Thurlby, Lincoln, England.

KIA-Killed In Action

Memorial to Resistance members who paid the supreme price, Chauny, L'Aisne, France. These brave men and women were called "The Army of the Interior."

Entienne Dromas at Marizelle-Bichancourt, September 1987.

John Neal and Bob Lindsay at the grave of their lost crewmember, tail gunner Vic Knox, killed when their plane was attacked. Taken at Couvron et Aumencourt Cemetery, 1994.

Josette and Serge Baudinot, Jean and Marie-Thérese Hallade, in front of the Cenotaph, Ottawa, 1988.

The "family" in Irvine, CA, 1991, in a photo taken by Neal. Shown from left are Josette Baudinot, Jean and Marie-Thérese Hallade, Bob and Lynne Lindsay, Monique Bauset, Jack Kupsick, Pierre Bauset and Serge Baudinot.

INDEX

CPSIA information can be obtained
at www.ICGtesting.com
Printed in the USA
LVHW091026121120
671515LV00022B/158

9 781681 621807